Redefining Student Success:
The Challenges and Implications of Extending Access

A Report on the College Board Colloquium

January 7–9, 2006
Dana Point, California

Redefining Student Success: The Challenges and Implications of Extending Access

A Report on the College Board Colloquium

January 7–9, 2006
Dana Point, California

The College Board: Connecting Students to College Success

The College Board is a not-for-profit membership association whose mission is to connect students to college success and opportunity. Founded in 1900, the association is composed of more than 5,000 schools, colleges, universities, and other educational organizations. Each year, the College Board serves seven million students and their parents, 23,000 high schools, and 3,500 colleges through major programs and services in college admissions, guidance, assessment, financial aid, enrollment, and teaching and learning. Among its best-known programs are the SAT®, the PSAT/NMSQT®, and the Advanced Placement Program® (AP®). The College Board is committed to the principles of excellence and equity, and that commitment is embodied in all of its programs, services, activities, and concerns.

For further information, visit www.collegeboard.com.

Contents

Welcome and Opening Remarks

Gaston Caperton, president of the College Board, led off the 2006 colloquium with a warm welcome and thank you to all those in attendance. "We are deeply honored to host such outstanding people in the education community."

Caperton referred to the recent Sago Mine tragedy in West Virginia, where he was once governor. "You probably see the people and the scene of this tragedy differently than I do. My father grew up in a coal mining town. I know these people have real courage and real character; they work hard, are patriotic, and care deeply about their religion and their families. They handle tragedies like these in quite a remarkable way. They have not had the educational advantages we have—but they go down into these mines every day so that their children won't have to." He referred to Michael Hooker, a former chancellor of the University of North Carolina, whose father worked in the mines and used his annual two-week vacation to take Michael, his only child, to visit colleges. "His father's life ambition was to see Michael go to college. These mining tragedies say a lot to me about how hard parents will work for a college education for their kids."

Caperton then spoke of the tradition of common woodpiles in West Virginia. "There were two rules: you put more wood back on the pile than you took, and you didn't play with fire near the woodpile. I fear our generation has taken more wood off the woodpile than we are replacing. When I think about what our parents did to make sure we could be where we are today, I think they always put more wood back on the pile than they took. If you look at our economy today, we are taking way too much wood off the pile by not saving, and running big deficits. Fortunately we have the largest economy in the world, but we can't keep taking that wood off the pile and not putting it back.

"The fires I see around the woodpile today are people's conversations about intolerant religions, the contentious political climate, a total disregard for world poverty, an expensive war." He referred to a recent article by Thomas Friedman, "Keeping Us in the Race" (*New York Times*, October 14, 2005), where he said that if we were really having a national conversation today about what is most important on the minds of most parents, it would be a loud conversation about why so many U.S. manufacturers are moving abroad—not just for lower wages, but to find smarter workers, better infrastructure, and cheaper health costs—and why our students are underperforming in the areas of math and science. Caperton said we should look at the numbers of engineering graduates being turned out in India and China compared to the United States.

"What has made America a great country is education. It is a commitment to excellence and equity, which is the mission of the College Board. We have to hold up our end of the bargain: take risks, have dreams that our students can do better, have high expectations, demand hard work, and yet be fair. We need to give all students an opportunity to get an education, so that they have a chance to live the middle class life that we admire and respect in this country. Yet we are failing in that in a remarkable way."

He concluded, "Each of us here has a meaningful job, a purposeful job, a job that makes a difference. Our jobs mean more now than perhaps at any other time in America. It's a tragedy like the one we have been seeing on television that makes me wake up and not take for granted what we are and what we have. We need to use this opportunity to focus on all the children and help them have equal access to education. Let's get rid of that fire around the woodpile—and put more wood on the pile than we have taken away."

Keynote Address:
Betraying the American Dream and Closing the College Gate

DR. GARY ORFIELD, professor of education and social policy at the Harvard Graduate School of Education and cofounder and director of the Civil Rights Project at Harvard, gave the keynote address. He began by seconding Gaston Caperton's remarks about how truly transformative a college education can be for students whose families have never connected to it before, and remarked that he was the first in his family to attend college.

In launching his address, Orfield stated, "We are going through a huge transformation in our society, and unfortunately we are going through it in a period of very weak leadership with very limited vision. The result is a major threat to our future." Orfield believes that if the situation is allowed to develop for a sufficient amount of time, it will create a very deep social and economic crisis. He sees the changing perception of the importance of education and the failure of policy (including the reversal of policies that worked well), especially in relation to the increasing diversity of the nation, as playing a major part in the development of this threat.

Orfield continued, "I will paint a picture that is frightening and deeply challenging." He sees a challenge ahead for educators to figure out what to do in their smaller circles as well as how to act as a community to change the discussion in the country and create an awareness of what needs to be done collectively to avert the crisis.

Orfield described where we are in the current transformation away from access and equity, indicating that the trends are currently more apparent in elementary and secondary public schools than in higher education. He presented a chart (see page 4) detailing regular public school enrollments by race/ethnicity and region in 2003-04. The chart reflects a declining number of white births, as well as the country's experience of the first major wave of immigration that is nonwhite.

Figure 1

Regular Public School Enrollments by Race/Ethnicity and Region, 2003-04					
	% White	% Black	% Latino	% Asian	% Native American
West	47	7	36	8	2
Border	69	21	4	2	4
Midwest	74	15	7	3	1
South	50	27	20	2	0
Northeast	66	16	14	5	0
Total	58	17	19	4	1

Source: Orfield, G. and C. Lee, (2006) *Racial Transformation and the Changing Nature of Segregation,* The Civil Rights Project at Harvard University. Cambridge, MA: President and Fellows of Harvard College.

Orfield pointed out that only 47 percent of the enrollment in schools in the western United States is white, not due to increased enrollment in private schools, but because white children are not being born. The country's population growth is coming from international immigration. "It is our first major wave of international immigration that is overwhelmingly nonwhite. The growth in the Latino population is especially striking." As for the Asian group, Orfield characterized it as split between very high achievers and those who are in refugee communities and face many of the same challenges as many Latinos. "We are in a transformative period; this is changing every year. We are only about a decade away from a predominantly nonwhite student body nationally, and the census projects that by the middle of the century our school-aged population will be only about 40 percent white.

"How can we make this work? How do we make a society with this racial and ethnic composition work fairly, when we have never had equal education in this country and, by a lot of measures, we are going backwards?" He told the group that in every part of the country, schools are becoming more segregated, not just by race and ethnicity but also by socioeconomics and language. This "triple segregation" is intensified by problems of transciency and the lack of health care for lower-income children.

These segregated schools have the highest percentages of inexperienced and uncredentialed teachers, and administrators leave as soon as they can move up. "These schools are judged as failures by No Child Left Behind." Many have "staggering" dropout rates. "In the typical high-poverty minority high school, where most minority students are now concentrated, less than half of the students graduate and almost none are graduating with the tools they need to be successful in college. We are responding to that by putting

in more exit tests from high school and more entrance tests for college, and eliminating remedial education in college."

Orfield pointed out that in 1976-77, there was even enrollment of whites, blacks, and Hispanics. Beginning with the Reagan years, there was a major cutback in student aid, and the Civil Rights Act was no longer enforced in higher education. In the 1990s, as the economy improved, black enrollment increased. There has been no real change in Latino enrollment in 30 years. "This is profoundly discouraging if you consider that the Latino community has more people who work full-time and are below the poverty level than the black community." If this is the case, "then you can't possibly afford to live in a place that has a good high school that can get your kid ready for college in a test-driven high-school-exit or college-entry environment."

Orfield stated that, while 17 percent of public school enrollment is African American, only 8.8 percent of B.A.'s awarded in 2003-04 went to blacks; of these, 66.7 percent went to women. "Given the fact that all the economic gains in our society since the 1970s have gone to people with college credentials, this tells you something tremendously important about the problems of African American families and communities." The situation with advanced degrees is even more pronounced.

Latinos currently comprise 19 percent of public school enrollment and are projected to be at least a third of public school enrollment by the middle of the century; by 2050, the Latino community, at more than 100 million, will be more than twice the size of the present African American community. Yet only 6.3 percent of the B.A.'s awarded in 2003-04 went to Latinos; of these, 60.7 percent went to women; and the situation with advanced degrees is no better.

"If you think about what this means for the future of our society, you cannot help but think that we are in really deep trouble. All of the population growth is from communities that are more or less excluded from higher education."

Orfield went on to outline the promise that once existed in terms of higher education:

- College for the poor: Pell Grants
- Tuition could be earned with a summer job
- Huge growth of campuses
- The civil rights revolution
- Declining real costs
- Open admission to four-year campuses

He outlined the "gigantic expansion" of educational opportunity in the United States after World War II. He described the GI Bill as "one of the best investments any country ever made in its future: our society was transformed by it." In the 1960s there was an explosion in educational opportunities with the expansion of community colleges; teachers colleges became state universities; universities became research universities. The 1965 Higher

Education Act for the first time provided federal financial aid for poor children to go to college. Upward Bound and other programs were designed to encourage and prepare for college the students who had previously been excluded. Head Start, Title I, Medicaid, Medicare, and Civil Rights legislation were all huge changes that made society much more equitable.

At the same time, Orfield noted, tuition costs during these years actually declined. Most students could go to a public university if they had a summer job and lived at home. Anyone with a high school degree had the right to go to a four-year college in most states. With what became the Pell Grant in the early 1970s (which actually covered much of the cost of a college education at that time), as well as these other societal changes and the increasing number of spaces available on campuses, "we had a promise that we could actually make college available—as we had made high school available a couple of generations earlier—to everyone. In the mid-1970s, there was a very brief period of equal access to college across racial lines among high school graduates." But, beginning in the late 1970s and early 1980s, and continuing to the present, tuitions have risen more quickly than family incomes, institutions have not funded access components, and cutbacks in state appropriations for higher education have reduced access to public institutions, where the great majority of students enroll.

Orfield then described current trends that he finds "really troublesome":

- Declining state and federal resources
- Large tuition and fee increases
- Transfer of aid from poor to middle class
- Retreat on civil rights
- Increasing reliance on tests
- Major cutbacks on remediation
- Vast transformation of population

"We have decided to shift the cost of education from the adult generation to the student generation, through loans and increases in tuition." This reduction in resources has led to the United States's slipping behind many countries in terms of initial enrollment in higher education. Orfield said that 1978 signaled the beginning of the movement of federal subsidies, from grants to students from low-income families to loans for middle-class students. There has been a dramatic decline in the percentage of college costs that a Pell grant covers, and the Clinton administration accelerated the trend of reduced access for low-income students with tax incentives for the middle class.

Orfield added that the retreat on civil rights began with the Reagan administration. "While the affirmative action battle has been won for the short term, there has been no significant enforcement of diversity among students and faculty for many years. In fact, some institutions are coming under fire from the Justice Department and the Office for Civil Rights for trying to maintain minority access programs."

The increasing reliance on college admissions tests has increased the stratification of college students between community colleges and four-year campuses, Orfield indicated. And remediation opportunities at four-year campuses have been cut back in 47 states. "This would be fine if all students had a decent high school to go to, that actually provided them what they needed for college." Many high schools, especially high-poverty high schools, are simply not preparing students for college. It "sounds good" to eliminate remediation at the college level—saving money and effort—but there has been no meaningful discussion of whether high schools are truly preparing students. "We have had almost no progress in the outcomes of high school education for a long time, and we have a growing dropout rate. We have a really big social crisis: We either have to get the students out of these schools, or do something about them—but instead we are sending more students back into these schools in the name of ending busing, or saving money, or having neighborhood schools."

Enrollment rates of Hispanic and African American students are not encouraging, and "completion is a much worse story than the access story." The black college graduation rate has very gradually increased. The Hispanic numbers are flat. In part this reflects the large continuing immigration of a population, with generally low educational preparation. "Nonetheless, they are our future labor force, our future citizens."

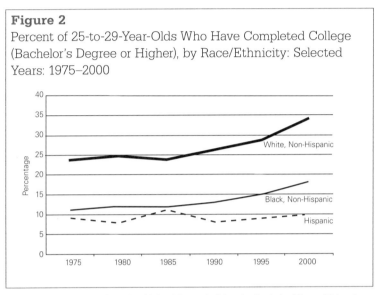

Figure 2

Percent of 25-to-29-Year-Olds Who Have Completed College (Bachelor's Degree or Higher), by Race/Ethnicity: Selected Years: 1975–2000

Source: U.S. Department of Education, National Center for Education Statistics, Digest of Education Statistics (2001), based on U.S. Department of Commerce, Bureau of the Census, March Current Population Surveys.

Orfield then shared data (see graph above) demonstrating that degree attainment is related strongly to income. "These educational premiums grew a lot in the last generation."

Orfield pointed out the big differences in college access based on socioeconomic status. "Tom Mortensen, who studies these issues a lot, estimates that if you are in the bottom SES (socioeconomic status) quartile, your chances of ultimately getting a college degree are about one-tenth the chance of those in the top quartile." Orfield sees the current higher education situation (particularly the reliance on standardized test results that have been shown to be powerfully related to parental income) as "ossifying" the social structure, given that economic opportunity is so closely linked to educational attainment.

The gap in college entrance between whites and other groups is growing. The movement of students, particularly minority students, to two-year versus four-year colleges, is problematic because so many two-year college students do not transfer and finish a four-year degree. There are major differences (often related to the income and racial/ethnic distribution of the surrounding area) among community colleges in terms of how many students ultimately earn a four-year degree. "We have to worry about whether we are reproducing at the higher education level the same kind of inequality that we see at the high school level. Given the projected population change, we need to do something about racial and economic diversity or we won't have any students."

Figure 3A

Changes in Access to Four-Year vs. Two-Year College, by Percentage

Race/Ethnicity	1972	1992	Diff.
White	69.2	59.3	-9.9
Black	73.7	55.1	-18.6
Hispanic	46.5	41.4	-5.1
Asian	N/A	61.7	

Social Class	1972	1992	Diff.
Top π SES	76.4	73.7	-2.7
Middle π SES	63.5	50.7	-12.8
Bottom π SES	60.5	36.8	-23.7

Source: U.S. Department of Education (1981, p. 61; 1996, pp. 12,21).

Figure 3B

Changes in Access to Highly Selective Four-Year Colleges, by Percentage

Social Class	1981	1998	Diff.
Richest (> $200K)	20.5	27.9	7.4
Upper ($100-200K)	14.8	17.3	2.5
Upper Middle ($60-100K)	8.1	8.8	0.7
Middle ($30-60K)	4.8	5.1	0.3
Lower Middle ($20-30K)	3.7	4.5	0.8
Lowest (<$20K)	3.0	4.7	1.7

Source: McPherson & Shapiro (1999, pp. 22, 23)
Note: The income figures are inflation-adjusted income defined by what they were in 1998.

Orfield also noted the race and gender gaps that exist in our society when measuring educational attainment and pointed to recent research that demonstrated the decreasing percentage of males (particularly among the nonwhite population) achieving higher education. "How can we have a society with stable families if men have no earning power and no status?" The Justice Department estimates that almost 30 percent of African American young men, and one-sixth of Latino young men, will end up in prison. Unfortunately, the public cost of incarceration is higher than that of higher education. For example, California spends more on its criminal justice system than it does on its higher education system. "No other society in the world today has decided to rely on imprisonment as a basic social policy. And a lot of this is about figuring out how to educate minority males…If we had an enemy who was going to steal our most important resource, and destroy our future, we would be mobilizing like mad. This is our most important resource. In a postindustrial society, the education level of the population is the only really important resource that's irreplaceable—and it is being threatened, and we are adopting policies that are actually making the threat worse."

Orfield then outlined briefly the income and cost gaps that exist in terms of paying for higher education, noting the recent trend towards merit-based aid (see Figure 4 below).

Figure 4
Institutional Grant Awards to Dependent Undergraduates in Public Institutions

	1992–93	1999–2000	% Increase
Total Dollars (millions)			
Need-Based	$423	$678	60
Merit	$677	1,283	89
Total	1,100	1,961	78
Number of Grants			
Need-based	317,000	448,000	41
Merit	334,000	490,000	47
Total*	621,000	896,000	44
*Average per Student***			
Need-based	$1,336	$1,515	13
Merit	2,024	2,618	29
Total	1,773	2,189	23

Source: Author's calculations from National Center for Education Statistics (2004a, 2004b).
*Total does not equal sum of need-based and merit grants, as some students received both types of award.
**For students who received a grant.

Orfield said that states have not been funding poor students or expanding opportunities for them—but they are giving merit awards to students who do not have financial need. Orfield believes that if states have enough money to cover the needs of the poor, and then want to give money on the basis of test scores, they might consider merit awards to the middle class; otherwise, it is an "unconscionable policy." Colleges and universities are following suit to remain competitive in the rankings. Most of the merit awards are going to students who would have attended college anyway. "Over 70 percent of white families have homes with equity that they can draw on, yet we exclude that as a college resource when calculating need. About 60 percent of minority families don't have homes, with equity to draw on; when they get a financial aid package with unmet need, it means the student can't go." Orfield also referred to the daunting prospect of applying for aid: "What is it like for families who do not own anything, have never taken on any debt, don't have any credit rating or banking relationship, to fill out these forms or find a loan agency to relate to?"

Orfield asked, "How can we turn this around? If we follow the existing pattern, we are in danger of having a generation that is going to be less qualified and less able to produce wealth than the generation that preceded it." Orfield expressed concern that the younger generation may well not be able to support the exploding number of older people who will be needing assistance. He reiterated that we are in danger of excluding the majority of our future citizens, and are reducing the safety net more and more. "If we increasingly stratify people, we will create an increasingly polarized society. It will be a society that will be very hard to govern. If a society becomes stratified enough, there will be a very explosive reaction.

"To this point, one of the great things about our country is that we have had a common dream: that we can get a decent house for our family to live in and send our kids to college; they can get married and raise their children in a safe environment. It is a dream that is the same across racial lines. If people start realizing that it's a lie, it will be a very major threat to our society. So far the dream has been held very deeply and steadily. It seems to me that everyone in higher education has a responsibility to make that real as much as possible."

Yet Orfield cautioned that year after year, because we don't get enough money from other sources, we are passing the costs along to students, and eventually we have different institutions and a different kind of society. "What we do to protect our institutions individually by keeping our faculty and programs going and keeping our rankings up and attracting good faculty, may not work collectively for our society." Orfield said we should acknowledge to society that "we really *do* believe in your dream, and we believe that it needs to be realized, and it will cost something, and we have to pay for it" through taxes and public investment. He urges the group to enter into the debate about what is necessary to have a decent public society, and into the debate about our relative priorities; for example, what is the cost of education as opposed to the cost of jails?

Orfield was encouraged by the mobilization of the higher education community around the issue of affirmative action. Colleges reached out and worked with business leaders, minority communities, and the armed services to explain that we could not have a viable society unless we could work across racial and ethnic lines. That was a huge accomplishment. But Orfield cautioned that we have other issues as well, such as changing the quality of high schools so that more students are prepared for college. Orfield outlined issues that need to be addressed: What is necessary to give kids in poor high schools a chance? Remediation is an investment, but a better investment than jail. We need to get enough support so that students can go to a public institution even if they are poor or working class. We have to look at the racial, ethnic, and social class consequences of our actions. "Our society is in danger of losing its promise, losing its mobility, and creating a generation that is less capable than others—and we are in a world where the costs of that failure will be huge. If we fail to do it, it will be seen as a much larger failure than anything that is happening to us internationally. It will make it impossible for us to maintain the role we have had in the world, which has been a powerful, creative, and very important role."

Orfield concluded, "There is not much that is more important than what you are discussing here at this colloquium." He urged the group to think about how to use their public, collective voice to explain to policymakers and communities the risks of where we are heading, and the possibilities that existed in the past and could exist again.

The audience then had a chance to respond. Richard Shaw, dean of undergraduate admission and financial aid at Stanford University, said, "The referendum movement puts forces into play such as those against affirmative action. Is this something that we could take on, to stop these countervailing forces?" Orfield responded, "What we have now is what the founding fathers feared and the reason they created such an indirect democracy. The issues are framed by one side of the debate, generally the side with the money to get the signatures. Affirmative action in California was outlawed by referendum without any real discussion. But elected officials at the state and federal levels, even in conservative times— other than in Florida—have never enacted anti-affirmative action legislation. So higher education professionals have to speak out in any way they can, to inject a democratic voice into a demagogic situation."

Keynote Speaker Bio

GARY ORFIELD is professor of education and social policy at the Harvard Graduate School of Education. Professor Orfield is interested in the study of civil rights, education policy, urban policy, and minority opportunity. He is cofounder and director of the Civil Rights Project at Harvard, an initiative that is developing and publishing a new generation of research on multiracial civil rights issues. Orfield's central interest has been the development and implementation of social policy, with a central focus on the impact of policy on equal opportunity for success in American society. His recent works include studies of changing patterns of school desegregation and the impact of diversity on the educational experiences of law students. In addition to his scholarly work, Orfield has been involved with the development of governmental policy and has served as an expert witness in court cases related to his research. He has participated as a court-appointed expert in several dozen civil rights cases, including the University of Michigan Supreme Court case that upheld the policy of affirmative action in 2003. He has been called to give testimony in civil rights suits by the U.S. Department of Justice and many civil rights, legal services, and educational organizations. In 1997, Orfield was awarded the American Political Science Association's Charles Merriam Award for his "contribution to the art of government through the application of social science research." A native Minnesotan, Orfield received a Ph.D. from the University of Chicago; he travels annually to Latin America, where his research work is now expanding.

Professor Orfield's principal publications include a series of reports on the national progress of desegregation during the past quarter century, and the following books: *School Resegregation: Must the South Turn Back?* (with J. Boger), 2005; *Higher Education and the Color Line: College Access, Racial Equity, and Social Change* (with C. Horn and P. Marin), 2005; *NCLB Meets School Realities: Lessons from the Field* (with G. Sunderman and J. Kim), 2005; *Dropouts in America: Confronting the Graduation Rate Crisis* (editor), 2004; *Racial Inequity in Special Education* (with D. Losen), 2002; and *Diversity Challenged: Evidence on the Impact of Affirmative Action* (with M. Kurlaender), 2001.

Second Day Welcome

Hal Higginbotham, president of collgeboard.com, welcomed the group to the eleventh annual colloquium on behalf of the College Board. "It's astounding to me to see how this event has grown and flourished. In an era in which so many—sometimes in our community but especially outside, in the press and among the general public—have become cynical about college admission, about gaming and self-interest, it is a useful counterpoint to take a look at the history of these events and the complex issues that they have engaged. All of you should be proud of your participation."

Higginbotham reminded the group of this year's theme, "Redefining Student Success: The Challenges and Implications of Extending Access." He suggested that perhaps what we are trying to do is to restore access, remarking that so many of those in the room were part of the halcyon days when there was a convergence of equity and opportunity. "We face a large-scale social crisis in terms of our educated workforce." Higginbotham believes it is up to higher education to save itself; the will to make the necessary changes must come from within. "The system in many ways works perfectly: we do have the world's best educational system, providing more quality of outcome than any system in the world…But there are real issues to address about student aspirations, family perspectives, academic preparation, and financing." Higginbotham sees sorting through these issues as a primary task of the College Board and its member institutions.

In stating the College Board motto ("connect to college success"), Higginbotham said we often think of that as students connecting to us—but that we should also think of how we connect to them. He went on to describe the "shared values" that are part of the College Board purpose:

- High Expectations: "For our students *and* for ourselves"
- Hard Work: "For our students, it means that achievement is not something that is gifted, but something that is gained, through hard work. It also means hard work for us; and the hardest work for us is finding ways to engage on issues like these, collectively."
- Fairness: "Especially if we look carefully at the statistics from Gary Orfield, we can easily see the risk in thinking that all is fair."

He concluded by urging the participants to "enjoy the colloquium, think, participate, and go home and engage your campuses and communities. We could not ask any more than that."

Youlonda Copeland-Morgan, vice president and dean of admission and financial aid at Harvey Mudd College, and chair of the colloquium planning committee, then spoke. She shared that her group chose the theme for this year's colloquium "because it is timely, it is relevant, it is necessary, and because people asked us to bring together individuals who can really help us make progress on the issues of access, diversity, and equity." She introduced her fellow committee members:

William Boyd, senior associate vice president of student services and budget administration at San Diego State University

Steve Brooks, executive director of the North Carolina State Education Assistance Authority

Georgette DeVeres, associate vice president of admission and financial aid at Claremont McKenna College, and chair of the College Board Trustees

Sally Donahue, director of financial aid at Harvard College

Mary Nucciarone, assistant director of student financial services at the University of Notre Dame

Shirley Ort, associate provost and director of scholarships and student aid at the University of North Carolina at Chapel Hill, and chair of the College Scholarship Service Council

Joellen Silberman, dean of enrollment at Kalamazoo College

William Wells, director of financial aid at Wake Forest University

She also singled out for thanks members of the College Board staff: Robin Casanova, Steve Graff, Kathie Little, Min Hee Kim, and Linda Peckham. They were treated to a round of applause. Copeland-Morgan also introduced Steve Brooks and Anne Sturtevant, director of financial aid solutions at the College Board, as facilitators of the event, handling the audience's response to the upcoming presentations and keeping programs on time. She also introduced Deb Thyng Schmidt, the writer of the proceedings booklet that will come out of the colloquium.

Defining Success: Overhauling Our Assumptions

Patricia Covarrubias, assistant professor of communications and journalism at the University of New Mexico, led off the panel discussion. She began with a bit of personal history. Having moved from Mexico to Davis, California, at the beginning of the third grade, she was placed in the lowest level class because she spoke only Spanish. "This was very painful for me, compounded by the fact that I did not have the linguistic ability to defend myself." Covarrubias set out to prove that she could learn and succeed. "I embraced assimilation, gave up my language, traditions, and cultural practices. It was never out of shame, but out of a sheer need to survive in a context that, if it was not intolerant of, was certainly inexperienced with, difference. So I reconfigured myself to conform."

Covarrubias described research she started three years ago while at the University of Montana at Missoula, which has an increasing number of American Indian students, "too many of whom will not complete their degrees because at that university, like many others, there is a 40 percent attrition rate among American Indian students." When she arrived on the campus, her childhood experiences came flooding back. She wondered if the only way for those American Indians to succeed would be to reconfigure themselves as she had, or if perhaps there was another way to succeed. With her background in the ethnography of communication, Covarrubias decided to use her skills as an interculturalist to conduct research to see if she could abstract a definition of academic success on behalf of American Indian students.

Covarrubias said that she is still conducting the research, so did not have final conclusions to report, but did have some key points to share. When Covarrubias asked students what academic success meant to them, Euro-American students replied along the lines of getting good grades, having a good GPA, graduating from college in four years, getting a job after graduation, etc. "While the American Indian students are very well aware of that paradigm for academic success, that paradigm is not theirs. It is in contradistinction to the broader cultural beliefs and values that they bring to campus."

Covarrubias indicated that at least six main themes have emerged in the data she is analyzing, but she wanted to focus on two dimensions that have become salient to the concept of academic success: goal setting and goal achievement, and self-transcendence.

Both Euro-American and American Indian students mentioned goal setting and goal achievement as facets of academic success; "I set my goal for a bachelor's degree and I am going to get there. However, from a cultural perspective, there is within goal setting and goal achievement a very important dimension of time, timeliness, pace, duration, as well as sequence, as well as breadth and depth. All of these are intermingled within American Indian conceptions of academic success as it pertains to goal achievement." Covarrubias shared a response she had from an American Indian student who was working on a master's degree in intercultural youth and family:

> "Academic success is having the ambition, determination, and will to keep plugging along. I don't really attribute good grades and a degree as academic success, although I think both play a role. I think what's more important is the commitment and devotion to overcome obstacles and barriers to earn an education. A student may not graduate, but their time in school has been a learning experience, and something to be proud of and to pass on."

Covarrubias pointed out how this response captures some cultural differences: the idea of the fluidity of time, of the nature of what should constitute academic success—learning—and about the outcome, how one measures success: passing it along to someone else.

For American Indian students, the temporal boundaries are intrinsic to the experience itself and not based on schedules imposed from the outside; the experience itself dictates and shapes what time should be spent. "How quickly one gets through school is informed by a life process that has its own natural timeline." Covarrubias shared a number of other responses that referenced the concept of taking things as they come without forcing life, including academic life, into a rigid timeframe, including this from a man who earned a Ph.D. in educational leadership: "…while pursuing a liberal arts education with minimal reverence to temporal limitations has assisted my wonderful journey, filled with roads which provided diverse perspectives, acquaintances, and experiences."

"It is not that American Indian students don't care about time, as I have heard said before; it's that they value time differently, it is prioritized differently, it should be allocated differently…Time for relationships takes priority over everything: time for family, for tribe, for community, for friends. And the practicality of what one learns is much more valued than the time it takes to learn it."

In terms of goal achievement, American Indian students felt that what they learned, based on where they started, was more important than grades. A man who recently received his master's degree in social work told Covarrubias, "I guess from where I came from to where I am now, I have already succeeded academically…I never thought I was going to graduate high school; I mean, at one point I never imagined myself even being in high school. And then I did that, so that was a success. And then just completing Freshman English: that was a success."

Covarrubias told the group that, for this population, doing one's best is valued. American Indian students see success in small steps. The culture values courage, valor, persistence, resilience, and hard work. Covarrubias urged the participants to consider these cultural values when determining whether to admit American Indian students, and also to think about how they can use these values to work for the students once they are on campus.

She then spoke of the idea of self-transcendence. While Euro-American students tend to see educational success as a way to enhance the self, American Indian students feel

academic success has not been achieved unless they transcend the self and give back to the community from their education. They ask themselves, "Am I making a commitment to the community? Am I helping other students?" The goal of their education is to help their family and their tribe. "The focus does not end with the growth of the self. These students ultimately want to go home and help." Covarrubias shared a number of quotations from American Indian students she interviewed, including this from one who was working on his doctorate in marine biology:

> "Academic success is achievement; it's achieving what you're going for, to achieve the goal. But my goals are to provide for my family and, with my degree, I plan to go back home and help my tribe establish a viable natural resources department, and that serves their needs."

Another student said, "Native Americans helping Native Americans is academic success." Covarrubias said that from these and other insights she gained from talking with students, "one can abstract certain important cultural values: generosity of spirit, loyalty to group, responsibility for the well-being of group, compassion. Not too bad as something to integrate with our system."

Covarrubias encouraged participants to compare the two definitions of academic success. "Euro-American students see and take a very linear, incremental approach to education, with parameters set externally. Native American students see themselves as contemporary warriors with obstacles to overcome. They see education as part of a larger journey that has many paths, marked by a complex, multifaceted set of 'growings' that need to occur: intellectual, personal, spiritual, sociocultural. And, finally, most important, academic success must transcend the self; it must be for the practical good of their people, the people with whom they are connected through wisdom, love, honor, respect, and compassion."

Amelia Katanski, assistant professor of English at Kalamazoo College, described her work as a member of the faculty admissions and financial aid committee. While the area of her academic expertise is American Indian studies—and particularly the impact of assimilation-era government boarding schools, whose philosophy was "to kill the Indian to save the man"—her focus at the colloquium was on the work she and her faculty colleagues are doing. Katanski said her faculty colleagues on the committee are committed to Kalamazoo College, but none of them are experts in college admissions and financial aid. She indicated she would share how faculty members "view, understand, and struggle with definitions of student success."

She then gave a brief description of Kalamazoo College: a liberal arts college with about 1,200 students, known for its strong academic reputation and the Kalamazoo Plan, or "K Plan," that incorporates challenging, on-campus liberal arts course work with career development, service learning, and study abroad opportunities. Over 85 percent of their students study abroad before graduation. A senior individualized project is required.

Defining Success: Overhauling Our Assumptions

"According to our admissions office, a prospective student is considered admissible if she or he possesses the appropriate academic credentials and is someone for whom Kalamazoo would be a positive experience. Because there are many more admissible students than spaces in the first-year class, we try to reward applicants who are 'best matches' with merit aid." Merit aid is awarded on the basis of academic and nonacademic criteria. The last time the criteria were fully evaluated was 1995, so the faculty committee was charged with reviewing the criteria, particularly nonacademic factors, to see if they are focused, useful, and still working for the college. "But if a 'best match' means a student will be successful at Kalamazoo, what do we mean by 'successful'? This question has been fascinating but frustrating to answer."

Katanski stated that their first step was to discuss their own definitions of success within the committee, and then to open the topic up to other faculty members. Through the process, they gathered "interesting, varied and, on some points, strikingly consistent narrative regarding student success at Kalamazoo." While this narrative is specifically linked to the college's mission and the K Plan, Katanski expressed hope that it would resonate with the participants, and similarities and dissimilarities among what her committee has found and what other institutions may see as student success can help further the discussion at Kalamazoo.

"When we asked ourselves and our colleagues 'what is success at Kalamazoo College?', the immediate answer actually mirrors what Patricia was saying her Euro-American students came up with." Among them were graduation in four years, or retention; but no one was content to rest with completing the degree as the definition of success. Likewise a high GPA was an initial answer that felt incomplete; she described students who master material and earn A's yet are not gripped by the topic, and other students who might not earn A's but are passionately engaged with the material and transform themselves.

So the faculty moved beyond these more typical definitions of success to compile the following "by no means comprehensive" list of characteristics of students they consider successful. They propose that successful students:

- are excited intellectually by everything and approach their work with purpose, energy, dedication, and excitement, whether or not they end up at the top of their classes;
- have a wide range of interests, but are able to dig deep as well as have breadth;
- connect their learning from one class to another;
- are self-led people who can take charge of their education, creating and constructing a life for themselves on campus and developing opportunities in addition to taking advantage of those that already exist;
- display curiosity;

- have what one faculty member described as "grit and traction to stay the course";
- have a willingness to move out of their comfort zones toward social awareness;
- are altruistic and do good works, not to break a record or win a prize, but because good works are intrinsically valuable;
- have a willingness to engage with faculty in an intellectual relationship;
- find an avocation, a direction in which to move with their interests, talent, and knowledge;
- appreciate diversity; and
- have a healthy balance between academic and nonacademic areas of their lives.

"Taking a closer look at these faculty-generated definitions of student success, we see that all of them could be boiled down to one significant concept, that of engagement. Further, all of them connect to our college mission statement, which is: 'Kalamazoo College prepares its graduates to better understand, live successfully within, and provide enlightened leadership to, a richly diverse and increasingly complex world.'" Katanski said they also relate to the "five dimensions" of a Kalamazoo education: lifelong learning, intercultural understanding, leadership, social responsibility, and career readiness.

Katanski went on to refer to the National Survey of Student Engagement (NSSE) administered by Indiana University's Center for Postsecondary Research in which Kalamazoo participates. The five benchmarks that NSSE uses to evaluate student engagement are level of academic challenge, student-faculty interaction, active or collaborative learning, enriching educational experiences such as study abroad or service learning programs, and a supportive campus environment and sense of community. "Our faculty-generated definitions, and the five dimensions, significantly reflect the NSSE benchmarks. It is striking how closely our faculty comments conform to those benchmarks on what engagement is." Katanski indicated that Kalamazoo students score well above the national mean and above the baccalaureate liberal arts college mean on four out of five of these benchmarks; and since both first years and seniors take the survey, one can see that Kalamazoo College has an impact on their level of engagement.

The faculty admissions and financial aid committee is now working to use the insights from their own list of characteristics, as well as the NSSE data, to develop an "engagement index" to help the admissions staff evaluate applications. Using work from another campus committee, which developed a list of knowledge, skills, and attitudes associated with each of the five dimensions of a Kalamazoo education, Katanski's committee's index asks evaluators to rank student achievement in each of the five dimensions on a three-point scale. The pilot effort focused on their own student advisees, whom they already knew well; they could determine if the student résumé and transcript effectively represented the "twinkle in the eye" of student engagement. They intend to use current merit-award students, and then a random sample of current students, to assess how well the index works. Once it is deemed effective and predictive of engagement, it can be used in determining merit aid for applicants.

Katanski shared that their efforts raise more questions than they answer. "Should success at Kalamazoo College mean shaping the incoming classes to constitute students who conform to what we already are as an institution? Or are we open to changing who we already are? How does our definition of success relate to these decisions and to issues of access as well?"

Katanski referred to a review article in the *New Yorker* (October 10, 2005), "Getting In: The Social Logic of Ivy League Admissions," by Malcolm Gladwell. He cites research by economists Alan Krueger and Stacy Dale, who say that "the character and performance of an academic class is determined to a significant extent at the point of admission." Katanski said Gladwell describes changes in Harvard's admissions policies in the 1920s (Harvard decided to consider character as a factor, rather than solely academic merit, in admission) and writes "You are whom you admit in the elite education business; and when Harvard changed whom it admitted, it changed Harvard." She indicated that Jerome Karabel argues in *The Chosen: The Hidden History of Admission and Exclusion at Harvard, Yale, and Princeton* that this decision was at least in part developed to exclude what had become an increasing number of Jewish students at Harvard. "This is an example of how we define merit or success as very much related to questions of access and student diversity." Gladwell also refers to a study by the Law School Admission Council, which found that engagement is high on the list of competencies that determine who would be a good lawyer, yet is not measured by the LSAT. "Gladwell acknowledges that an admissions process that is searching for good lawyers is 'necessarily going to be subjective, because things like passion and engagement can't be measured as precisely as academic proficiency.'" Gladwell indicates that sometimes subjectivity in the admissions process is the only way to provide "the social outcome we want."

"At Kalamazoo, how can we address our need and desire to work toward a more diverse campus environment through the process of defining student success? How can we look for and value factors that might help us to shape our merit aid and thus, in some significant ways, our incoming classes, so that they help us to become who we want to be as an institution? These are the kinds of questions our committee continues to struggle with, and we depend on your wisdom and expertise to help us answer them."

Deborah Bial, president and founder of the Posse Foundation, indicated that the three panelists were there because they wanted to show how success can be defined in some nontraditional ways. The Posse program started in 1989 after a minority student told her he would not have dropped out of college if he had had his "posse" with him. This sparked the idea of sending a team of students together to a college.

Posse started with one group of students at Vanderbilt. Vanderbilt ran the students through their traditional admissions process and predicted they had about a 20 percent chance of making it through their freshman year. They would not have admitted the students through their traditional process: They attended high schools Vanderbilt did not typically recruit from; they had SAT® scores that did not look like the SAT scores of the general student body. "But they took a chance on a program with no track record, and needless to say we

graduated all those students and they went on to do amazing things. Since then, we have identified over 1,500 Posse students. They have won over $140 million in leadership/merit scholarships from our partner institutions, and they are persisting and graduating at a rate of over 90 percent. So Posse is doing something that is working, and we are identifying young people who typically would not be connecting to your institutions."

Bial outlined Posses's three goals:

- To expand the pool from which the best institutions of higher education are recruiting young people

- To help the institutions that already are committed to diversity make the campus climate feel more diverse; to change the campus climate so that it becomes more welcoming to students from every background

- To make sure Posse students graduate and become leaders in the workforce, representing the true demographics of this country at the tables where the decisions get made

"Posse has become probably one of the most comprehensive college access and support programs in the United States, because we aren't just a pipeline program, we don't just find kids. We support them all the way through college." Bial outlined the four components of the Posse program, focusing on the first component because it is the most related to the panel topic:

- The Dynamic Assessment Process (DAP): This recruitment strategy was designed to help find students that colleges would want but who would not show up through regular routes. Posse reaches out to high schools and community-based organizations, guidance counselors, and teachers, who then nominate students. In the five cities where Posse operates (Boston, Chicago, Los Angeles, New York, and Washington, D.C.), 6,000 students were nominated this year for 300 Posse slots. The students went through three months of screening, beginning with large group, three-hour interviews of 100 or so students where staff assess noncognitive traits. The standouts get called back for a second interview (before grades are looked at) that is a more traditional behavioral one-on-one interview. And then they look at the traditional information to sort down to the final group. For each of the 23 partner colleges, twenty students are identified who will apply to the college with the intention to enroll if admitted. Admissions staffers meet with the candidates as a group and observe them in dynamic situations. Posse staff then sits with the admissions staff to help determine which 10 would make the best Posse for that institution.

- An eight-month precollegiate training program, focused on leadership development, teambuilding, diversity, and academic success (including a writing component)

- A four-year on-campus program with mentors, retreats, campus visits, and liaisons

- A career program that connects Posse students with internships and careers

The audience had a chance to respond. Jim Belvin, director of financial aid at Duke University, asked, "Does Posse work only with schools that provide merit scholarships, or are you willing to work with schools that take the position that they will meet full need for any of your students who are admitted?" Bial responded that they work with schools that provide merit scholarships, although most of their students do have high need and are getting aid they would have received anyway. "But that is a conversation we would have with you."

Bill Wells, director of financial aid at Wake Forest University, asked Covarrubias how her research has influenced how she evaluates students in her classes. "For example, how would you grade a student who demonstrates a high level of subject mastery but evidences no personal growth or vice versa? How does your approach square with external or societal expectations?" Covarrubias responded, "Evaluation is always the unpleasant part, at least for this instructor. The best way to answer whether to measure by finished product or to measure by effort is to say that for me it is not an either/or but a both/and approach. I have a lot of communication with students throughout the term, and especially at the end of the term. I have redesigned assignments so that they tap into student strengths, so that failure is not automatically built in. I also assign a lot of group work. And I involve students in their own evaluation. In the case of American Indian students, I understand the cultural constraints that might keep them from coming to see me, so I find ways to connect with them."

Cynthia Gutierrez, AVID Coordinator at the San Diego County Office of Education, asked, "How do Posse students access the program? And are there criteria in order to stay in the program?" Bial reiterated that students are nominated; and to remain in the program, they need to meet the requirements of the partner institutions.

David Jones, associate dean for admissions at the University of Texas Medical School at San Antonio, asked, "Are Posse students also successful at the next levels of study after college?" Bial replied, "These students are unbelievably successful and very ambitious. They have gone on to be lawyers, doctors, and other professionals. They may have a bumpy start at undergraduate schools, but they are incredibly smart and ambitious and look like other graduates of their colleges by the end of four years."

Academic Preparation: A Barrier to Access and Success?

Jenny Krugman, executive director of partnerships at the College Board, led off the discussion with a description of a project the College Board has undertaken with the state of Florida. Krugman urged the group, "Take what you see and what you hear and connect it to what you do. Those of us at the College Board and those of us in other organizations across the K–12 landscape have real, live solutions for the goals that you carry forward every day."

The goal established by the governor of the state of Florida in 1999 was to increase the number of minority students attending institutions of higher learning; to increase Advanced Placement Program® (AP®) participation and performance for underrepresented students; to increase the number of students exposed to higher learning through the PSAT/NMSQT®; and to increase the number of teachers trained to teach advanced courses. To that end, the state provided funding to cover the cost of the PSAT/NMSQT for all tenth-graders; provided greater incentives and efforts to increase minority AP enrollment and reduce disparities between minorities and nonminorities in AP course offerings; and implemented a strong teacher professional development program to include Summer AP Institutes and scholarships for AP training.

Krugman stated, "The AP program is a great program, providing quality control countrywide. Because of this quality control, you can know how you are doing as a student, as a teacher, and as a school. What Dr. Orfield told us last night is sadly true: There are really three Americas in K–12 education: those stellar schools, with tons of AP courses and all sorts of opportunity; there are schools that are adequate; and there are schools that are sad places. The AP Program and the publication of AP scores bubble up these truths."

Krugman indicated that every year in Florida, because of the partnership between the College Board, the community college system, the state department of education and the four year university system, more than 2,000 professionals—superintendents, principals, counselors, and AP teachers—are trained. The College Board offers 1,000 scholarships each summer to potential AP teachers: first to minority teachers, and then to those working in schools with underrepresented students, and then to beginning teachers in order to broaden the group of teachers who can inspire students.

She shared the following results of the Florida Partnership:

- While overall AP participation has increased more than 125 percent, minority participation has risen 128 percent, from 2000 to 2005.
- AP performance has increased 102 percent for the number of AP Exam grades of 3 or higher (including a 103 percent increase for minority students).
- Between 1999 and 2004 the number of tenth-grade students taking the PSAT/NMSQT has increased 269 percent for the general population and 402 percent for minority test-takers.
- Between 2000 and 2005, there has been a 65 percent increase in the number of minority students taking the SAT.
- From 2000 to 2005, there was a 35 percent increase in the number of SAT takers accompanied by a 1 point increase in SAT verbal scores.
- While the number of African American SAT takers increased 47 percent from 2000 to 2005, mean SAT math scores increased 2 points.
- While the number of Hispanic SAT takers increased 84 percent from 2000 to 2005, mean SAT verbal scores increased 2 points.

Krugman said that they review the data daily. "A big piece of the partnership is the AP program because that speaks to colleges." She also pointed out that the mean math scores for African American students and mean verbal scores for Hispanic students increased, even with the increase in the number of test-takers.

Krugman reported that there has been a striking increase in the number of sophomore PSAT/NMSQT takers since the inception of the partnership. But, because there is not a state mandate to take the SAT, there is a different story. Evidence of the push for AP curricula and the mandated sophomore PSAT/NMSQT is obvious, as is what happens when the PSAT/NMSQT is voluntary for juniors. Krugman says the SAT numbers are creeping up since the establishment of a test-preparation piece in 2003. "This tells every parent in the audience that students will not necessarily make academically rigorous choices for themselves, so it is up to us to focus on rigor."

Krugman said she was proud to announce that "the Latino achievement gap has been buried for two years." The leading subgroup for mean SAT scores has been Hispanics for the past two years. The percentage increase in the raw number of African American students taking AP classes is the greatest of any state in two years; "this in a state that had not before the late 1990s prided itself on high achievement or equity issues."

In concluding her remarks on the Florida Partnership, Krugman stated, "What the College Board does in its connections across the country with grades 6–12 is to work with the fabric of education. Giving the PSAT/NMSQT is not enough; it is the data that spools from that assessment that is key. We have been remiss in K–12 in not creating the fabric that ties together real teaching and real learning. Top schools have fabric; bottom schools don't." Yet in serving primarily the weakest 90 of the 400 senior high schools in Florida, great progress has been made through the partnership.

Krugman then went on to describe a partnership undertaken by the College Board with a particular school district in North Carolina. This district with "a lot of fabric" set a goal to increase student achievement on state assessments and increase participation in AP courses, especially among minority students. The superintendent of the district declared use of his own AP Potential™ tool. AP enrollment was mandated for ever-larger numbers of students. The PSAT/NMSQT is given to all tenth- and eleventh-grade students in the district; each principal's AP offerings are monitored; a strong pre-AP program was created; and a strong teacher professional development program was implemented.

Krugman urged the participants to get behind the new emphasis on AP at the College Board: that AP courses are for all students. "We mean it because it is rich and powerful and heretofore has been open to a tiny group of mostly suburban, mostly white students."

Krugman shared results of the district partnership:

- Minority participation in AP has risen 56 percent.
- Overall participation in AP has doubled.
- Even as the overall number of AP students has grown, 5 percent more students (including 5 percent of all minority students) are receiving grades of 3 or higher.
- The percentage of students receiving a grade of 3 or 4 on the state's algebra end-of-course assessment has risen by 5 points.
- Even as the number of students taking the SAT has increased, average grades have risen by 1.8 percent since 1999.
- The largest increase in SAT participation was by African American students.

The results show that "it's about saying you want it to happen and then following it up with measurement, accountability, and fabric."

Krugman pointed out the increases in the number of district students taking the state assessments who scored at or above expectations, and the decline in the number who scored below expectations.

Finally, Krugman described a partnership between the College Board and a particular school. The goal at this school was to increase student achievement on the FCAT (Florida Comprehensive Assessment Test) and increase participation in AP, especially among underrepresented students. The school worked with the Florida Partnership and colleagues to increase enrollment in AP courses, especially for underrepresented students.

Again, the results were overwhelmingly positive:

- AP participation has increased 454 percent from 2000 to 2005, with an increase of more than 635 percent in the number of AP Exams taken.

- The percentage of African American eleventh- and twelfth-grade students participating in AP increased from 4 percent in 2000 to 35 percent in 2005, while the percentage of Hispanic eleventh- and twelfth-grade students increased from 4 percent to 32 percent.

- The percentage of sophomores taking the PSAT/NMSQT has increased from 4 percent in 2000 to more than 80 percent in 2004.

- More than 50 percent of seniors enrolled for 2004–2005 took the SAT as compared to 43 percent for seniors enrolled for 1999–2000.

Krugman concluded, "I urge you in higher education to think of ways to enter into a marriage with the K–12 community in your home city to build more powerful schools and to allow principals, teachers, and superintendents to see the value of rigorous academics." She mentioned research done by Wayne Camara (vice president of research and analysis at the College Board) and other research that shows that secondary school academic rigor is more important to student achievement in college than SAT/ACT scores or GPA, especially for minority students. "Help us as we lead a rise to a rise in rigor. You can become the point persons, the clarions."

David Armstrong, chancellor of community colleges and workforce education for the state of Florida, spoke next. He described the self-analysis the Division of Community Colleges and Workforce Education has pursued for the past year and a half, "trying to understand the issues of access and student success in our state." He indicated that in Florida they are fortunate to have comprehensive data on students, from pre-K through graduate school. They can examine the exact courses students take, whether they are on the free or reduced-lunch program or not, and other characteristics; they are able to track student progress at

all levels. In particular, they have looked at data on the entire ninth-grade cohort from the 1996-97 school year (200,000 students) for seven years, into their second year of college. And they have looked at national data for benchmarks. As part of their research, they have been testing assumptions and doing a policy audit, such as: "How well are we really doing in terms of access and success? Are the policies working or are they serving as barriers to student success? What are best practices?"

Armstrong referred to a report by Patrick Callan, president of the National Center for Public Policy and Higher Education, two years ago, describing waves of higher education access, growth, and expansion. The current students are much more diverse, much poorer, and far less academically prepared to succeed in college.

Armstrong outlined the situation facing college-bound students, nationally and in Florida.

> He shared information from *Cracks in the Education Pipeline* (Committee for Economic Development; www.ced.org/publications/subject.shtml):
>
> - Nationally, low-income students, who are less likely to take a vigorous course load in preparation for college, are also less likely to enroll in college.
>
> - Twenty-three percent of low-income students graduate from high school and enroll in college, compared to 38 percent for all students.
>
> - Seventy-three percent of less-qualified, high-income students enroll in college compared to 69 percent of more-qualified, low-income students.

He also cited Clifford Adelman's 1998 report, *The Kiss of Death? An Alternative View of College Remediation*, which found that students who have a challenging college preparatory curriculum at the high school level, regardless of grades, are usually better prepared to do college-level work. Armstrong went on to say that there is a common perception in higher education that about 60 percent of all students go on to some college. While it is true that about 62 percent of students who graduate from high school go on to college, Armstrong cautioned (based on data from *Cracks in the Education Pipeline*) that, of a given 100 high school students, 33 do not complete a high school diploma in four years. Twenty-nine who do complete a diploma do not go to college. So only 38 of 100 students go on to college within the first year after completing high school and, of that group, only 18 complete a bachelor's degree (in Florida, the comparable number is 14; in Massachusetts, 28 complete the degree). Armstrong shared other information: only 8 percent of students from a low-SES (socioeconomic status) background take a rigorous course load compared to 28 percent of high-SES students. Eighty-six percent of students from high-SES backgrounds qualified at least minimally for some type of higher education.

Academic Preparation: A Barrier to Access and Success?

Looking at the 200,000 ninth-graders they have tracked in Florida, Armstrong said that only 44 percent of those in the free lunch program went on to any higher education, as compared with 58 percent of students who were not in the program. In terms of college preparation, 82 percent of those who took Algebra I or less as the highest level math course they completed needed remediation at community colleges. If students took Algebra II or anything higher than that, 63 percent were prepared to go on to college-level math work.

Focusing on Florida, Armstrong shared these findings:

- About one-third of Florida public high school graduates will attend a community college the year following graduation.
- About two-thirds of them will need at least one area of remediation.
- Students needing any type of remediation are less likely to earn a certificate or an associate degree than those not needing remediation; only 8 percent will receive a certificate or a degree.

"In Florida, unlike most states, all students who need remediation or developmental work must receive that developmental work at a community college. About two-thirds of those entering community college in Florida need at least one remediation course; about 60 percent need mathematics."

Armstrong noted a number of factors that contribute to the situation in Florida. "There is a lack of alignment between high school graduation requirements and assessments and college entrance requirements and placement assessments. What is being measured in each of these assessments is different; the state department of education is working in an effort to create alignment in requirements and assessments." He also outlined other contributing factors: a tendency to take less rigorous courses in high school; a feeling that college is "not for me"; family income plays a very large role.

He listed outcomes if nothing about the current system changes:

- Students will continue to complete high school unprepared for postsecondary education.

- Community colleges will continue to spend time and resources teaching remedial education to prior-year high school graduates.

- Completion rates will remain lower than they should or could be.

- Society and individuals will not be able to benefit at the level they should.

Armstrong then shared a number of options for turning the situation around, working with K–12 partners, working systemwide, and working within particular institutions:

- Encourage students to take advantage of acceleration mechanisms such as the AP Program and Dual Enrollment.

- Share research on the relationship between high school courses taken and success in postsecondary education.

- Support programs that encourage middle and high school students to plan for postsecondary education.

- Encourage immediate transitions from high school to college.

- Help high school students understand that postsecondary education is for them, not just the "other" students.

About 35,000 Florida students are enrolled in dual enrollment classes that colleges offer in conjunction with K–12; they have seen similar increases in college access and college success as with the AP Program Krugman described. "Sixty-seven percent of dual-enrollment students graduated with an associate degree within three years, compared with 55 percent who were not dual-enrolled. African American and Hispanic students succeeded at an even higher rate. It's not just that they're getting higher-level courses, but that there is engagement between these students and someone from a college who helps them believe they can go on to college."

Armstrong said that federal programs, as well as the College Board partnership Krugman described, have resulted in many support programs, including funding for community colleges to form relationships with high schools and to mentor students from low-performing schools. He mentioned specifically a program for high-risk middle school students, who are offered a contract with a prepaid scholarship plan that will cover tuition at a community college or four-year state college if they stay in school, graduate, and stay out of trouble; each of the students is provided with a mentor to work with them through high school. "The success of this program has been tremendous. More than 15,000 students have gone through the program since 1990; and 91 percent of participants have graduated from high school and gone directly to college."

Armstrong then shared some options the community college system can use within itself to help change the current situation. "Our research has caused us to enter into meaningful conversations on our campuses on a variety of topics, including the issue of withdrawal from classes at the college level. The average number of withdrawals by campus ranged from one course for all who graduated to eight courses. There is a good correlation between those colleges with a high course withdrawal rate and lack of graduation. So why are we letting so many students withdraw from courses? What is the responsibility of students, faculty, and staff in this process?"

Armstrong's division also studied a course, Student Life Skills, that about half of their community colleges are offering. "It is an entry-level exposure to what it means to be a successful college student. Lots of study skills are built in, since many students never learned how to handle rigorous courses. The students enrolled in these classes have a 15 percent higher rate of success than students who did not have access to this program."

Armstrong's team have used the Community College Survey of Student Engagement, which looks at the impact of faculty and staff engagement with students, and the degree to which they challenge students and engage with them outside of class. All students in community colleges in Florida took the survey. "More than anything, that caused our faculty and staff to reassess what they were doing. They learned that while they thought they were engaging all the students in their classes, they found out that they were not. We hope this will stimulate greater retention and success."

In conclusion, Armstrong said there was one major factor that they identified more often than anything else. "We often think that if we only had more money, we could be better at retention and success because we would have a lot more programs. We found that some institutions with fewer resources actually were the most successful." They did a case study comparing two very small community colleges that are similar in terms of student demographics, size, and resources; but one was much more successful in graduating students. "In that institution, there is leadership and a culture that focuses on student success. We have been focused a lot on access—we need to focus as much or more on student success. When *leadership* makes it a priority, it is possible to make a big impact."

The audience then had a chance to respond. Michael Behnke, vice president for university relations and dean of college enrollment at the University of Chicago, said, "It's nice to come to a conference and hear some good news. What are the barriers to replicating a partnership like the one in Florida in more states? In connection with that, does No Child Left Behind help to energize or synergize the process?" Krugman responded that NCLB is "helping us find our failures. As a solution, it is potentially as good as anything we have had—we can't hide the schools that have not been achieving. As for state partnership barriers, partly it is a lack of faith on the part of school leaders in themselves. We need to have faith that our students and our teachers can do it if we show them how." Armstrong added, "It takes leadership at the beginning to commit the resources and set goals." Krugman said, "It also depends on the politics, how secure the state and school leaders

are, what the union and nonunion positions are. There needs to be a willingness to work across the party line, to create a tapestry and a fabric."

Barry McCarty, dean of enrollment management at Lafayette College, asked about focusing on middle schools, which could make a big difference in terms of preparation for college. Krugman replied, "Middle school is the Achilles heel of American education, and for the College Board. The College Board is beginning to address this issue. CollegeEd® is a middle school program, working to get underrepresented students to understand college as a concept. It is very specific about what you have to do to be well prepared; they write essays and résumés about who they are as scholars. Springboard™ has just begun as the pre-AP program for all children. These sophisticated concepts have to happen before the ninth grade. In Florida, we have started putting some middle school teachers into Pre-AP® training, and sending some to the AP Summer Institutes, so they can think about how to prepare middle school students for advanced course work."

Jim Bauer, assistant dean of enrollment management and director of financial assistance at the University of Miami, said, "You talked about the gains that have been made. I was looking for a more substantial gain within a population. What it looks like is that we have a ratcheting up, but there is no real gain on the low-income students in terms of the percentage who are taking the test; there is still a disparity between the two groups." Krugman responded, "That is absolutely true; we have not eliminated the achievement gap. I'd like to give you a local example, given the university you represent. Of the 400 high schools in Florida, 90 are extremely low performing, and 17 of those are in the Miami-Dade district, of which your city, Coral Gables, is a part. We are in those schools with consultants all the time. We have made a lot more progress with African American, Latino, and low-income students in the high-performing high schools. We can overcome the achievement gap in strong schools, but we have not yet figured out how to overcome the gap in the weakest schools." Armstrong added that the high schools in the lowest income areas cannot get the best teachers and resources, and the students are not exposed to higher-level course work. Krugman concluded, "We are trying to build a culture of excellence in these lowest performing high schools, getting the superintendents and principals to work with us."

Mary San Agustin, director of financial aid and scholarships at Palomar College, said, "I work at a community college. You mentioned working with faculty to be accountable to help lower the withdrawal rate. The withdrawal rate is highest in the first term. How would you recommend we work with faculty to address this, to be proactive?" Armstrong replied, "First, create a culture of evidence. We gave faculty the data, the evidence of what's happening. We have four institutions participating in the Lumina Foundation's 'Achieve the Dream' project, developing ways to work with students who want to withdraw from classes. Tallahassee Community College has focused on the bottom 25 percent of students. Every time one of them wants to withdraw, there is encouragement of that student by a staff member in addition to the faculty member. We work to find a solution for the student's issues, which are often financial as well as academic."

Julia Padgett, university director of financial aid at Emory University, said, "We have the Hope Scholarship, which is politically popular. Florida has Bright Futures. Did you meet any resistance or arguments about getting into the fabric of these low-performing schools?" Armstrong said, "Our Bright Futures program, which is supposedly a merit program, has very low requirements of a 3.0 GPA and 1000 on the SAT. Ninety-five percent of entering freshmen at the University of Florida qualify, to the tune of $350 million, a third of the entire state funding for the community college system budget. Seventy-five percent of those receiving Bright Futures scholarships could well afford the very low tuition at our state colleges and community colleges. The program has done little to promote additional access. We are using that as a way to describe what the real need is, using it as a way to show that more need-based aid is necessary."

Redefining Success for the Global University:

The Challenges and Implications of Increasing International and Study Abroad Enrollments

Ron Moffatt, director of the International Student Center at San Diego State University, led off the panel by describing recent developments in the enrollment of international students in U.S. higher education. He said he would speak from two perspectives: first, from his role as a campus practitioner; and second, from his role as board member and incoming president of NAFSA: Association of International Educators.

Figure 5

Redefining Success for the Global University U.S. Trends 1954–2002

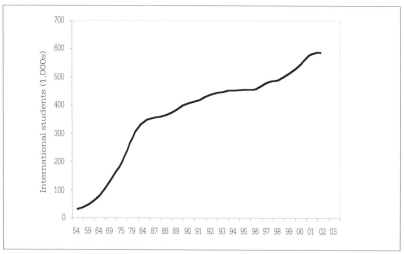

Source: The Institute of International Education

He began with information from the Institute of International Education. The United States saw steady growth as the destination of choice for international higher education from 1954 to 2002. "Our attraction had a lot to do with our reputation for offering the best product on the market. Our reputation is well established; a 2004 report by the Institute for Higher Education Policy on the academic ranking of world universities lists the United States as possessing 17 of the top 20 universities in the world. Most students I know attributed their reasons for coming here to the belief that a U.S. higher education would provide them a first-class ticket into the vanguard of the global workforce." International student enrollment grew about 5 percent each year and, in 1992, the United States attracted a 42 percent market share of the world's mobile students. "That was the high-water mark of our market dominance."

The years 2001–2004 saw the first decline in more than 30 years in international student enrollment, with a 2.4 percent decline in 2003–2004 and an additional 1.2 percent decline in 2004–2005. Among those institutions enrolling 1,000 or more international students, 43 percent saw a decline. "What was once a $13 billion revenue stream for the U.S. economy and the source of much coveted revenue for our campuses began decreasing and heading south.

"Not surprisingly, leading opinion makers have taken notice, and we are creating more public awareness" in the media. College administrators have tended to blame these declines on post-9/11 regulations as well as on negative perceptions of the United States following the increase in regulations, which has tarnished the reputation of the United States as an open and welcoming society. "It is the case that students, who constitute only 2 percent of all foreign visitors to the United States annually, are the most heavily monitored and controlled group of any visa category." Moffatt believes there is a lot of work to be done to restore the country's reputation and image, and that simply reducing the regulatory obstacles, as the government is working on now, will not be enough.

"But," Moffatt went on, "I venture the following proposition: the United States would have experienced similar declines even if 9/11 had never happened. The decline might not have been so precipitous, but the real forces leading to it were already in motion well before 9/11."

Why is the United States slipping in enrolling international students? Moffatt referred to what he terms a "Grand Slam Triple Play":

- The "first out" Moffatt believes, is that we are pricing ourselves out of the market. "Tuition, fees, and living expenses for international students continue to skyrocket, and there are few sources of aid or counterbalances at the institutional or federal level. At my institution, prospective international students must demonstrate that they have $25,000 parked in a bank somewhere for each year of study. This is unimaginably difficult for those being paid in pesos or rupees or dinars."

- The "second out" is that we are the leading competitor in this market, but we are not competing. "While competing nations work to remove disincentives to study in their countries, our national policies actually exacerbate the disincentives to study here. Our competitors decided they, too, want to reap more of the benefits international students bring, and they have developed policies and allocated resources to facilitate access to their higher education institutions. Their strategies worked: their market share grew while ours shrank."

- The "third out" is that we lack a comprehensive international education policy. "What exists instead in Washington, despite the best efforts of many talented advocates, is a disarray of conflicting priorities between State, Education, Commerce, and Homeland Security that systemically thwarts interagency cooperation in advancing a comprehensive international education policy."

Moffatt went on to describe who our competitors are and what they are doing. Currently, the majority of international enrollment is found in these five countries:

United States	28%
United Kingdom	12%
Germany	11%
France	10%
Australia	9%

Figure 6
Current Players

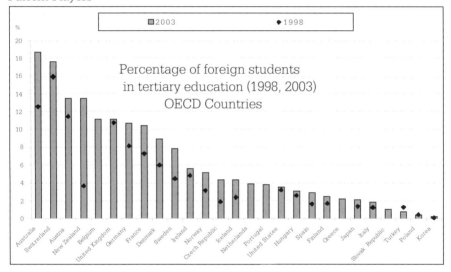

Source: The Institute of International Education

"What's interesting about our current competitors is how rapidly some of them have expanded their capacity for foreign students. In this five-year period (1998–2003), many made big percentage changes."

Moffatt said the new competitors are just emerging. They are attracted to this market because of its predicted growth. The international higher education student market is expected to grow fourfold in the next 20 years, from 1.8 million to 7.2 million. "In response, there has been a surge in institutional capacity to capture these students, and stronger competition for a greater share of the global mobility market." Some of the emerging competitors are current competitors who are banding together in regional collaborative programs; some traditional feeder countries are investing heavily in higher education to keep their students at home; and some are "innovative upstarts" featuring branch campuses at U.S. institutions or multinational e-learning communities.

Moffatt described the collaborative process in Europe. Europe established the Bologna Process in 1999, seeking to link European universities into a single system by 2010, offering three-year bachelor's and two-year master's degrees. Increasing numbers of European universities are offering programs taught in English. In 2001, Europe produced 40 percent more engineering and science doctorates than the United States. Eastern European countries are heavily marketing their higher education to non-European Union (EU) students based on its low cost compared to Western Europe. And a number of European countries are working together to market education to non-EU students.

"However, the real engines accelerating the capacity boom are the same engines that are currently sending us close to 60 percent of our international students: Asian countries." Moffatt went on to describe China, where the number of undergraduates and doctoral holders increased nearly fivefold in 10 years. China graduates four times as many engineers as the United States. State money for higher education has doubled since 1998; in 2003, it was $10.4 billion. And the number of foreign students studying in China has more than doubled since 1998—from 43,000 then to 110,000 in 2004. There are more Korean students studying in China this year than in the United States.

As for India, for the last three years it has sent more students to the United States than China, "but that soon will change." Their economy is rapidly growing, opening up knowledge-based employment opportunities. Both private and public sectors are making a heavy investment in the higher education infrastructure. "They are providing viable options for their best students to remain at home."

So how should we respond? Moffatt cautioned that it would take a lot of effort from a lot of people to effectively deal with these driving forces. First and foremost, he called for progress in Washington. "There is currently more supportive rhetoric for international education coming from Washington, couched in terms of national security, U.S. economic competitiveness, and U.S. leadership. We can also expect to see a continuing patchwork of proposed regulatory reforms aimed at clearing the latest clog in the pipeline." While Moffatt sees this as nothing revolutionary, he expressed hope that legislation may be written that would significantly improve the playing field, exempting student visas from Section 214(b) of the Immigration and Nationality Act. "If passed, it would dramatically change how student visas would be issued and would create an entirely different image about our country's openness to foreign students."

Moffatt also recommended more professional networking. NAFSA, with 9,000 members worldwide, can be an advocate for international student enrollment and help with training, professional development, and networking opportunities. He encouraged the group to take advantage of their resources.

Additionally, strategic planning is necessary. "This is probably the most important step you can take to ensure the success of your own international enrollment plan. Make sure your

international applicant pool is strategically developed—meaning you have clear objectives compatible with institutional priorities and supported by the key players."

Finally, Moffatt suggested that it might be time for a redefinition of success. "To what extent do our international student enrollment strategies incorporate rationales that go beyond numbers, rankings, and revenue streams? How do our plans for enrolling international students tap into strategies that will optimize intercultural connection, engagement, and learning both in and out of the classroom?" What kind of innovative partnerships can we build on our campuses, in our local communities or regions, and neighboring states, or in other countries, that will facilitate student mobility in ways that advance our campuses' capacity to prepare global-ready graduates? How can we create new learning communities that effectively integrate e-learning processes with global competency outcomes? And to what extent do our institutions assume responsibility for fostering global citizenship?

Jane Edwards, director of international programs at Harvard University, spoke about U.S. students studying abroad. "I enjoy talking about study abroad because, generally speaking, it is a pretty upbeat topic, because it generates so much excitement among young people. The advising process for students who are considering significant international experience is one that is filled with astonishing possibilities and which, in most cases, is ultimately crowned with success. For that reason, it is particularly important that we try to figure out ways to make study abroad as inclusive as we possibly can and reach as many members of our student body as we can."

She quickly reviewed statistics about study abroad for credit, with data from the Institute of International Education (which Edwards said is available in the *Open Doors Report on International Educational Exchange* at www.iie.org). "Study abroad numbers are growing, unlike international student participation in the U.S." In 2004-05, 191,321 American students studied abroad. While this was a 9.6 percent increase over the number for 2003-04, and double the number who studied abroad a decade ago, the *percentage* of participation has not really grown; it still represents only 1 percent of all postsecondary students, or 2 to 3 percent of college graduates nationwide.

The majority of students studying abroad (96 percent) come from four-year schools and are Caucasian (83 percent); African Americans make up 3.4 percent, Latinos 5.1 percent, Asians 6 percent, and Native Americans 0.5 percent of those studying abroad. "What does the fact that the majority come from four-year schools suggest about the way in which access to an international experience may be differentiated from the very beginning by the type of institution that students are studying at?"

Study abroad students go overwhelmingly to Europe. "We are sending very large numbers of students to four countries in Europe, and that picture has not really changed."

But there is growing interest in Latin America, at least in part because more and more students are learning Spanish. There has also been growth in the numbers going to Africa, Asia, and the Middle East.

Figure 7

Study Abroad in the Twenty-First Century Where Do Students Go?		
	2002-03	**2003-04**
Africa	2.7%	3.0%
Asia	5.6%	6.0%
Europe	62.9%	60.9%
Latin America	15.3%	15.2%
Middle East	0.4%	0.5%
North America	0.7%	0.6%
Oceania	7.3%	7.4%
Multiple Regions	5.1%	5.5%
Total Students	**174,629**	**191,321**

Source: Open Doors Report on International Educational Exchange

"In terms of when students study abroad," Edwards stated, "the message is that longer-term study abroad is declining and will continue to decline; the growth is in the shorter-term programs. Because of the ease of travel and because of the problems that many students face in getting away for a semester or a year, we will see a proliferation of short-term experiences."

Edwards also indicated that three themes are relevant to the national discussion of the importance of international education:

- Globalization
- National Preparedness
- World Peace

"Globalization has been discussed on campuses at least since the 1980s; it is now on the rise again because of a perception that the world has changed radically. If the world has changed so much, what do we need to do to prepare our students? I am constantly asked what global competency means. My definition comes from Richard Lambert, who wrote about this topic 20 years ago. He concluded that one needs a combination of skills and attitude, which

amounts to an understanding of the language wherever you are, area knowledge, empathy, and an ability to understand that somebody's differing point of view might have value. I think the final question related to global competency, especially for this administration, is: 'Can you perform the necessary tasks in an intercultural situation?'"

As for world peace, Edwards said, "I have a very different attitude toward what I think I am doing with students, beyond global competency. I am asking myself the question, 'What is the nature of an interior life that will make somebody have within themselves the qualities that they need to be happy at this particular moment in history?' My belief is that, since, if you don't go anywhere, globalization will come to you, the ability to manage diversity is one of the things that can prepare you very well for the future. There have been three waves of development of study abroad: one between the two world wars, one just after World War II, and the current wave that began in the 1970s. The wave after World War II was about peace; the Fulbright program was about peace, understanding how other people live and how they feel, about learning from people and teaching them at the same time. We don't hear much about that today."

As for national preparedness, the current Lincoln Commission was established by the Secretary of State to develop a new national scholarship program, the Lincoln Scholars program, with the goal to put one million American undergraduates abroad within the next 10 years (see www.lincolncommission.org for more information). "But their report title page states, 'What nations don't know can hurt them.' It goes on to talk about the need for national preparedness, just as Ron already mentioned: economic competitiveness, national security, and U.S. leadership. There is nothing in there to suggest that this is about the desire to live more harmoniously on the planet."

Edwards then spoke about issues of access as they relate to opportunities to study abroad. While 70 percent of high school students believe that they will study abroad, few actually enroll and participate in these programs. "Access is really about collaboration across campus." Edwards outlined some of the stumbling blocks to enrolling more students:

- **Money:** Money issues include not just financial aid, but institutional fee structures, the investment an institution makes in study abroad, what programs will receive credit, and how programs are structured and priced. For example, if students need to work full-time while they are in school, how can they go abroad during the academic year? Edwards believes institutions should plan programs strategically, as an institutional commitment: crunch the numbers and then develop programs that will work for students and the institution.

- **Structure:** In some cases, the needs of the curriculum preclude study abroad, especially in the sciences. Professional attitudes also exacerbate this: Some medical schools will not accept courses for credit that were taken abroad. Timing and external commitments and institutionally specific obstacles can be problems.

- **Culture:** The home culture of the student can impact access. Some students have obligations to their family—or their posse—to provide support, or they come from families that never traveled or spoke of travel as a valuable experience. Edwards sees lots of opportunity for outreach with this group. Attitudes at the institution and athletic or extracurricular obligations can be barriers. Lack of information can also be a barrier, though, in some cases, there is so much information that it is like having none. It is important to target the information toward the groups that most need it. Finally, fear can be a factor for students and especially parents: We have become much more fearful as a society since 9/11, and it has had an effect on student access to programs.

Edwards then quickly shared what she sees as "waves of the present in study abroad."

- Curriculum Integration: finding courses abroad that are essentially the same as courses here.

- Assessment of outcomes and of the quality of the experience abroad: making less-anecdotal, more-qualitative data available regarding the value of international study.

- Recognition of experience abroad outside the classroom: finding ways to recognize service learning, volunteer activity, internships, and other activities abroad as having a value that parallels that of study abroad.

- Questioning the impact of U.S. programs on host environments: Classrooms abroad are becoming more and more like those in the United States. "It would be a real shame if we get to the point that we are sending a million students abroad only to discover that there is no 'abroad' to send them to."

The audience then had a chance to respond. Joe Russo, director of student financial strategies at the University of Notre Dame, asked Moffatt for the source of his statistics about international students coming here. Moffatt responded that it was primarily from a NAFSA report by Rachel Banks, "The Explosion of Higher Education Capacity Abroad," and from OECD (Organisation for Economic Co-operation and Development) data. "There are so many breakdowns in the data that I hesitated to get into too much detail in the presentation; I would also refer you to the data in "Open Doors."

Henry Ingle, vice chancellor of instructional services, planning and technology, and online education programs at San Diego Community College System, asked, "What options are there for students who attend community colleges to study abroad? The types of programs developed at four-year colleges often do not fit with the issues and aspirations of community college students." Edwards responded, "This is a huge problem. The models do come from the four-year liberal arts college model. There is more time in the four-year curriculum, and also students are less tied into dealing with their external life. We need to work on short programs that are integrated with term programs, and how to finance those. The problems are money and conceptualization."

Mary San Agustin asked two questions about financing. "What is the average household income for students studying abroad from Harvard?" Edwards deferred the question to Janet Irons, associate director of financial aid and senior admissions officer at Harvard, who said they have done some research on this, and those studying abroad are representative of the range of incomes for Harvard students as a whole; there is the same average family income for students studying abroad. San Agustin continued, "We have a low-income population, and going abroad is an extra expense for our students. So the only ones who can go are middle-income students, and when they do go, they have to take out loans to offset the cost of living." Edwards added, "We haven't even begun to solve this problem. For the most part, not enough questions have been raised about it. In four-year colleges, the financial aid structure takes care of it; that is not the case in community colleges, and it's a huge impediment."

San Agustin then asked Moffatt, "Is NAFSA seeing a trend in terms of scholarship availability for international students since 9/11? I have donors who are becoming more sensitive about non-U.S. citizens getting scholarships." Moffatt said, "The financial assistance for international students really comes from their own sources. There is no federal assistance. Private scholarship money is rarely focused on international students. What is available to them is graduate assistantships, so many of our international students go to community college first to save money. Eighty-five percent of our undergraduate international students transfer in from community college."

Julia Benz, director of student financial services at Rice University, said, "I am curious to hear more about e-learning. Is the importance of study abroad related to having your body in a different country?" Edwards said, "If there is no possibility of going somewhere, there is value in videoconferencing. We can use it to open up opportunities for communication among young people, which really can be extremely powerful." Moffatt added an anecdotal example, "We have an accounting professor who brought together people from Thailand, Switzerland, Peru, and San Diego for a class via teleconferencing. As a result of the class, all six of the U.S. students who participated studied abroad the next year."

Margaret Drugovich, vice president of admission and financial aid at Ohio Wesleyan University, asked if research shows whether international alumni have institutional loyalty. Moffatt replied, "The private schools are way out in front in terms of developing international alumni, particularly the schools that have had large enrollments. State schools need to work on it more effectively; it takes an enormous amount of time and effort and has to be ongoing. University of California is a model for doing it well."

Mabel Freeman, assistant vice president for undergraduate admissions and first-year experience at the The Ohio State University, said they had recently held a Big 10 conference on international education. "We recognize that there are some countries that have a need to send students out because they do not have the capacity, and we need to get good information so that we can develop strategies. We also face the challenge, as public universities in the Midwest, of explaining the Midwest to international students. We recognize the need to work together to explain the benefits." Moffatt added, "There are regional aspects to recruitment. But I find that the best recruitment method is by word of mouth. Good service on campus is the best thing you can provide, in terms of recruitment of future students."

Cynthia Hartley, director of graduate student aid programs at Stanford University, said, "Sometimes it is difficult to see students come back from study abroad less changed than I would like to have seen. How do we evaluate what a significant change is?" Edwards responded, "We have seen some transformative experiences, as well as others who are just the same when they come back. We need to try to figure out what the factors are that result or don't result in those kinds of changes. We rely on a lot of self-reporting as the basis, as well as data from the study abroad staff. It is a data collection problem that the field has been working on for years. There are also some things we can do better to provide adequate preparation for students who are going abroad to facilitate attitudinal change."

David Charlow, executive director of financial aid and senior associate dean of student affairs at Columbia University, asked, "Have you seen trends in exchange programs?" Edwards replied, "I want to set up undergraduate exchanges at Harvard because it sends a message of reciprocity, a message of the belief in the possibility that someone else's university might be as good as yours. From that perspective, exchanges are an important thing to do. But if it is a direct exchange and the students must pay the same as any student attending your institution, it can hamper recruitment." Moffatt added, "Our experience with exchanges includes 30 or so that work if the faculty make it happen. They send an important message. But they are very labor intensive, and there are financial equity issues. We find organizations like ISEP (International Student Exchange Program), a consortium of 135 universities worldwide, very helpful. If you send five out, they send five in. They do the mechanics; you just admit them and find housing."

Pam Horne, assistant to the provost for enrollment management and director of admissions at Michigan State University, said, "We have one of the largest study abroad programs in the country in terms of sheer numbers, not necessarily percentage. I really appreciate Jane's comments about accessibility in terms of short-term experiences. We have freshman seminars abroad, including ones before students come to campus. Talking about these programs with prospective students is exciting. So we are working on making programs accessible in terms of money and length. We have families whose students are first-generation who are more positive about two weeks abroad with credit awarded than a whole semester or a year abroad; it also lowers the fear factor. We also think that freshman study abroad helps in terms of student success and retention."

Tally Hart, director of financial aid at The Ohio State University, added, "OSU set a goal of having an equal number of study abroad students from those groups who have the money and those who do not. We did not have new money to add, but what we did was move a financial aid officer to the study abroad office at those times when they were getting the most information requests. We found this had a profound impact, so that students could get information about academic and financing aspects of study abroad at the same time. We have much more interest than ever before, and greater access to study abroad."

People and Jobs on the Move:
Implications for Higher Education

James H. Johnson Jr., the William Rand Kenan Jr. distinguished professor of management at Kenan-Flagler Business School, and director of the Urban Investment Strategies Center, Frank Hawkins Kenan Institute of Private Enterprise at the University of North Carolina at Chapel Hill, shared research he has conducted over the past decade. "The findings document a set of rather profound demographic and economic changes that we are currently experiencing as a nation. The message that I hope you will take away today is as follows: The way the world does business is changing rapidly and dramatically, and America needs to move rapidly to equip itself to compete successfully in the global marketplace. Higher education can play a critical role in preparing our increasingly diverse society for the new world economy—but *only* if it transforms itself into a more nimble, entrepreneurial, and catalytic agent for change."

Johnson spoke of two key demographic forces first. One is what he terms "the 'browning' of America, the increasing role that nonwhite ethnic minority groups are playing and will continue to play in the growth of the U.S. population. The browning of America is driven in large part by both legal and illegal immigration." He shared a series of slides outlining this growth.

Nationally, 77 percent of the net population growth from 1990 to 2000 was attributable to nonwhites; Johnson indicated that the 127 percent increase in nonwhite population in the Northeast was because that region was a net exporter of whites during the same period. This trend has continued since 2000.

Johnson said, "Because the nonwhite population is much younger and has a higher fertility rate than the white population, most population projections forecast that the nonwhite population growth will outpace white growth until 2050. There will be about 375 million in total population at that time. Consistent with my concept of the browning of America, note that the white population is projected to grow by only 29 percent during this period, while the black, Native American, Hispanic, and Asian/Pacific Islander groups are projected to increase by much larger percentages."

This will result in a major color adjustment in America's population:

Figure 8

America's Color Adjustment		
Race/Ethnicity	**1995**	**2050**
White	73.6	52.8
Blacks	12.0	13.5
Hispanics	10.2	24.5
Asian	3.3	8.2
American Indian	0.7	0.9

Source: McCloud (1996)

Johnson then spoke about the increasing diversity in terms of geographical redistribution.

Figure 9

U.S. Total and Foreign-Born Population Change, 1990–2000			
	2000 Population	**Absolute Change 1990–2000**	**% Change 1990–2000**
Total	281,243,499	33,323,643	13.4%
Foreign Born	32,989,429	11,472,676	53.3%
Hispanic (Foreign Born)	114,410,703	6,331,264	78.4%
Hispanic (Native Born)	20,760,734	7,057,303	51.5%

Source: Public Use Microdata Samples, 1990 and 2000 (5% samples)

"Undergirding the increasing diversity of our population is a massive geographical redistribution of population, which is driven mainly by immigrants and Hispanics. The U.S. foreign born, the foreign-born Hispanic, and the native-born Hispanic populations all grew more rapidly than the total population during the 1990s. This trend occurred in varying degrees of intensity in all regions, including the South." At the state level, the majority of the foreign born are still concentrated in the major immigrant gateway states. But Johnson indicated that other states experienced significant foreign-born population growth in the 1990s, much of it driven by Hispanics.

Johnson said that some of the most rapid foreign-born growth occurred in metropolitan areas, indicating a trend of relocation from the major gateways to places where one would not have expected them to locate in the past. This redistribution trend is driven by employers looking for labor in certain fields: poultry and meat processing, the hospitality industry, and construction.

"As a consequence of these demographic shifts, colleges and universities will have to re-engineer the business of education to accommodate an increasingly diverse applicant pool. Between 2000 and 2050, the traditional college-age population is projected to grow rapidly, but the growth will not be evenly distributed across racial and ethnic groups. Paralleling shifts in the total population, the white share of the traditional college-age population will decrease from 65 percent to 44.6 percent. The nonwhite share will increase to 54 percent in 2050, from 34 percent in 2000. Among nonwhites, the greatest growth will occur among Hispanics, whose share of the traditional college-age population will increase from 13.8 percent to 28 percent."

Next, Johnson spoke of the second major demographic force he sees—"the 'graying' of America: the growing share of the population that is 50 or older."

The baby boomers and immigrants to the United States who were born during the baby boom years have swelled the U.S. boomer generation to 84 million. Over the next 15 years, approximately 12,000 people per day will turn 50. Within the next five years, this demographic surge will begin aging out of the labor market. It will be a significant exodus, with enormous implications for the human resource needs of public and private sector organizations, including higher education.

Figure 10

Absolute and Relative Change in the Gender/Age Composition of the U.S. Population, 1990–2000			
Gender/Age	2000 Population	Net Change 1990–2000	Percent Change 1990–2000
Total	281,421,906	32,712,033	13.2%
Male	138,053,563	16,814,145	13.9%
Female	143,368,343	15,897,888	12.5%
Age 18–34	67,035,178	-2,878,520	-4.1%
Age 35–54	82,826,479	20,024,490	31.9%
Age 55–64	24,274,684	3,126,761	14.8%
Age 65+	34,991,753	3,749,922	12.0%

Source: 1990 U.S. Census; 2000 U.S. Census

"Annual applications for retirement benefits are projected to increase from about 1.6 million in 2003 to about 3 million annually in 2023. This exodus is important, because the baby boom was followed by a baby bust. The native-born population, especially native-born whites, stopped having children in sufficient numbers to replace themselves. We have not replaced ourselves in the labor market. Largely for this reason, one study forecasts a U.S. labor shortage of about 10.6 million by 2010. To give you a sense of the dramatic difference in fertility behavior, if you look at native-born women aged 14–44, they have about 61 live births per 1,000 women; foreign-born Hispanic women have 112 live births per 1,000 women."

In the late 1960s and into the 1970s, there was a dramatic expansion of higher education to accommodate the boomers, leading to a surge in new faculty hires. These faculty members are rapidly approaching retirement age. Johnson warned that colleges and universities will have to develop succession plans to address the aging faculty challenge. He shared data from the University of North Carolina at Chapel Hill as an example of this trend. "Roughly two-thirds of the faculty members are aging baby boomers. Not all will retire at one time. But how do you replace 30 percent or 66 percent of your faculty? The competition for faculty members will be intense. There will be pressure to diversify the faculty, given the increasing diversity of the student body. Graduate schools will have to work with undergraduate minority students to encourage them to go into Ph.D. programs."

Johnson then turned to the magnitude of recent economic and employment shifts. In the first wave of globalization, blue collar jobs went overseas; this began in the 1960s and continues to the present day. "Nationally, 5.3 million manufacturing jobs have been lost to globalization since 1979; roughly half of this loss occurred between July 2000 and July 2003."

Many of these workers went back to school to retool for white collar jobs in the information economy. But, in the early 1990s, Johnson explained, those jobs began to move overseas in the second wave of globalization. First, U.S. firms outsourced work related to the upgrading and maintenance of their computer programs. During the late 1990s, the trend accelerated as firms outsourced work to address Y2K programming needs. More recently, in an effort to cut costs in the latest recession, U.S. corporations have engaged offshore vendors in what is termed "business process outsourcing" involving a range of business functions. Johnson said some state government contracts are even moving offshore, particularly call centers for benefits information.

Now higher-order, knowledge-intensive work is moving offshore; knowledge process outsourcing is growing. It is most evident in financial services institutions, such as banks, insurance companies, mutual funds, investment firms, and credit card companies. Johnson said this is projected to grow rapidly.

While these figures indicate that 11 percent of jobs are at risk of outsourcing, Johnson suggested 14 percent are vulnerable if figures for higher-end medical work ("medical tourism" for procedures done offshore) are included.

Johnson said that most economists tend to downplay concern about outsourcing. They think the United States will demonstrate its usual resilience and develop the next wave of leading-edge jobs. But Johnson warns that three recent trends affect our ability to bounce back.

- "First, the global competitive landscape is changing dramatically. Consider the developing nations that are embracing capitalism and free trade: China, India, and the former Soviet Union. Collectively, they have 10 times our population and produce more well-trained college graduates each year than we do. And their graduates perform the same work as educated American workers for about one-tenth the cost. They have also created a business and regulatory environment necessary to compete with the United States."

- "Second, immigrants to the United States have constituted much of the talent pool that has driven innovation in our economy. At the undergraduate and graduate levels of higher education, international students and the children of immigrants are responsible for almost all the enrollment growth in the physical sciences, math, and engineering programs, which are incubators for new job creation. But security restrictions since 9/11 have threatened our ability to attract the next generation of innovators."

- "Third, U.S. firms are beginning to shift research and development offshore. For example, General Electric has established an offshore research and development facility, the John F. Welsh Institute, in Bangalore, India. They have filed more than 150 patents since 2000. The average Ph.D. scientist there earns $650 a month. How can we compete in the United States with those numbers?" Johnson continued with information about medical research and development. Many U.S. headquartered multinational companies are moving research and development operations to India. He pointed out that "medical tourism" is on the rise and described the case of a North Carolina resident whose heart bypass surgery at the University of North Carolina would cost $200,000; in India, it would cost $6,750, including the round trip, surgery, and recuperation in a resort. And there is a lower mortality rate in hospitals there than in any hospital in the United States. "That is the changing landscape."

"What does this offshoring of research and development mean for higher education? It may mean less research and development money flowing to colleges and universities from the private sector in the years ahead. And it may not be realistic to assume that the federal government will fill the void. Federal research dollars as a percentage of the GDP have remained flat for the past 15 years. The offshore movement of white-collar jobs will put pressure on colleges and universities to accommodate a growing number of adults who will need to retool and upgrade their skills in order to compete for new jobs." One can see signs of this likely increase in the latest long-term unemployment statistics:

Figure 11
Percentage Increase in Long-term Unemployment, by Education, 2000–2003

Education Level	% Change
High school or less	156%
Some college	259%
Bachelor's degree or higher	299%

Source: Economic Policy Institute (2004)

"The adult population will drive the demand for continuing, lifelong education in the future. Part of this growth will be the boomers, in search of intellectual as well as skill revitalization. The retirement age for college graduates is decreasing. Traditionally aged students can benefit from these older students. There will be a powerful, mutual benefit to colleges to enroll the niche market of wealthy retirees."

How can higher education respond to these challenges? Johnson proposed a number of strategies:

- **Redouble recruitment efforts** even in the face of a parent group of college graduates who may be unemployed or underemployed.

- **Reengineer admissions policies** to better reflect the changing population; however, the socioeconomic status of the most rapidly growing segment will pose major challenges. Higher education institutions will need to devise strategies to increase college participation rates of the underrepresented minority groups; create innovative scholarship and financial aid packages to underwrite their education that do not violate U.S. law regarding racial and ethnic preferences; and provide the requisite academic support and mentoring to ensure successful matriculation and graduation.

- **Appeal to Congress to reconsider impacts of post-9/11 immigration reforms** to enhance our ability to recruit talented students, especially at the graduate level.

- **Develop an education access model based on inclusivity rather than selectivity,** including methods to address an increase in older learners as well as more diverse students.

- **Devise a comprehensive succession plan to address the baby boomer problem,** including a strategy for retaining high-potential young talent, especially persons of color, from within the existing ranks, and an aggressive worldwide search for diverse talent.

- **Transform universities into entrepreneurially oriented economic engines** to address U.S. employment losses. Higher education institutions need to move away from their inward-focused, "ivory tower" orientation and become more outwardly focused entrepreneurial engines for new business development and job creation. This will require changing the faculty reward structure to embrace more equally traditional basic research and action-oriented research.

- **Restructure curriculum with an emphasis on "intellectual entrepreneurship"** with an eye toward teaching students to become more resourceful and innovative in creating solutions to domestic and international problems. Students will need to graduate with entrepreneurial acumen and a willingness to take high risks for high rewards, and to be resilient and tenacious.

- **Adopt entrepreneurial fund-raising strategies:** Administrators will need to become institutional entrepreneurs in order to generate resources to attract the best students and faculty, and to transform their campuses into innovation engines of job creation and societal benefit.

"It is only through the embrace of such a broad definition of entrepreneurship that higher education institutions will create economic, artistic, social environmental, and other types of value in the years ahead. The most successful and competitive universities can turn adversity into opportunity and deal with internal challenges and external threats. They can do this by developing, nurturing, and unleashing the full entrepreneurial potential that exists on campus. It will ensure that graduates can compete successfully in the knowledge economy of the future."

The audience then had a chance to respond. Karen Fooks, director of student financial affairs at the University of Florida, said, "As for how higher education needs to be more responsive, it seems like a golden opportunity for for-profit education. Do you see this as the slow death of the traditional liberal arts education?" Johnson said, "Yes, I am afraid I do. Universities do have to respond to the challenge of outsourcing because we have an obligation to our customers. Yes, a liberal arts education is all well and good but, at the end of the day, a student needs a job. You are competing globally with some really smart competition."

Joe Russo said, "In regard to the liberal arts, one of its strengths is that it helps people to adjust. It helps people think clearly, analyze, and communicate. The better those skills are, perhaps the better the opportunity to adjust to a changing environment." Johnson responded, "I hope you can convince corporate America that that's the case; that's the challenge."

James McCoy, associate vice president for enrollment management, at Xavier University (Ohio), asked, "In entrepreneurial higher education, what is the role of faculty management, i.e., tenure?" Johnson replied, "There is already talk about doing away with the tenure system. If you look carefully, you'll see that there are two tiers of faculty emerging on most elite campuses. Increasingly, the teaching load is carried by adjuncts and instructors. That is a foreshadowing of the way the trend is going to shift."

Margaret Drugovich stated, "I have read recently that some economists think these vast discrepancies in worldwide salaries will eventually equalize." Johnson cautioned, "Not in our lifetime. There is a race to the bottom. You can go a long time in China before you get to the bottom. And if it is not about salaries, then the rate of technological change will continue to remove jobs. I am not convinced that it will equalize anytime soon."

Judith Lewis Logue, director of financial aid services at the University of San Diego, asked, "How will parents find out about this?" Johnson said, "Some parents are very aware of what is happening; they are the ones who are losing their jobs. These global forces are impacting them."

Wendy Beckemeyer, vice president of enrollment management at Alfred University, asked, "Given what we see in terms of Hispanic families moving to unexpected places, will this mean that Hispanic students will be more mobile than they have been in the past?" Johnson said, "I think students will be highly mobile. And some states are aggressively moving to get these mobile Hispanic students. For example, Iowa has just rebranded itself as the new Ellis Island of the Midwest. It is all about aggressively recruiting because they have an aging demographic. But we do have to get past all this 'undocumented' stuff that we seem to be focused on."

Alison Segal, college counselor at Highland Park High School (Chicago), said, "My school is highly Latino. Many students are undocumented. What is their future in terms of higher education access?" Johnson said, "My philosophy is based on the demography and the numbers; I think we would be crazy not to make every effort to educate undocumented kids. We are an aging population, we have not replaced ourselves, and we are aging out of the job market. Why would we want to leave students here uneducated? They are not going to go 'home.' Fifty-five percent of them were born here. It becomes a form of enlightened self-interest to invest in the education of these kids."

Henry Ingle asked, "What are the quick things we can do as institutions to respond to what you have described?" Johnson said, "Number one is that we cannot make the argument for increasing diversity in higher education on social and moral grounds; we need to make the business case. Second, we need to make the case in strategic places—to our boards of trustees and chancellors, and throughout our institutions. And we need to address the aging baby boomers: how we can recruit people to replace them."

Dan Goyette, director of the office of student financial aid at Marquette University, said, "We heard earlier that the perception of the American dream is still alive. Globalization may signal that that reality is changing. What can we do to help kids with the fact that this is not the case?" Johnson responded, "I run an after-school program for students from concentrated poverty communities. One of the major challenges is to keep up hope on the part of young people. Our commitment is to show up every day with the same message. You have to build trust and be consistent with your messages."

The Perfect Storm: The Financial Dilemma Facing Middle-Income Families Accessing Higher Education

This panel was composed of Sally Donahue, director of financial aid at Harvard College; Tally Hart, director of financial aid at The Ohio State University; Don Honeman, dean of admissions at the University of Vermont; Heather McDonnell, director of financial aid at Sarah Lawrence College; Stuart Oremus, director of college counseling at The Wellington School; Bill Schilling, senior director of student financial services at the University of Pennsylvania; and Joellen Silberman, dean of enrollment at Kalamazoo College.

Donahue described the intention of the panel to discuss among themselves how to deal with the middle-income dilemma for families accessing higher education, and then to open it up for audience participation. "First of all, what exactly is middle income? The answer is: It depends on where you're sitting, and what you're facing in terms of expenses. The national median income is $63,000; for Harvard families, the average income of need-based grant aid recipients is $90,000, well above the national median."

Donahue indicated other issues that get involved in the middle-class dilemma: public and private sticker prices and net prices in relation to family income; rural middle-income students versus urban middle-income students; issues of class; and family circumstances. "Defining and meeting need is a complex process and somewhat of a moving target." The ramifications of a consumer society are part of the mix; she referred to a recent article in the *Economist* about the inability of the very, very rich to have status "marker" items because those with less income are taking on debt to acquire those same items. She also mentioned that the national savings rate is 1 percent, including retirement savings: "So much of the savings is inaccessible to families for financing education."

Donahue then shared data from the College Board's *Trends in College Pricing*. The first chart gives data about what has happened in terms of sticker price and net price over the past decade at public colleges. "This is not a truly alarming trend, but it has become more complicated given the spending patterns of families."

Donahue then shared data about net price as a percentage of family income, at both public and private colleges.

Figure 12:
Net Price: Published Tuition and Fee Charges Compared to Tuition and Fees
After Average Grant and Education Tax Benefits Per Full-Time Student, Public
Four-Year Colleges and Universities, in Constant (2005) Dollars, 1995-96 to 2005-06

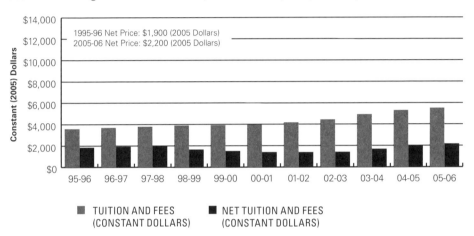

Figure 13:
Net Price: Published Tuition and Fee Charges Compared to Tuition and Fees
After Average Grant and Education Tax Benefits Per Full-Time Student, Private
Four-Year Colleges and Universities, in Constant (2005) Dollars, 1995-96 to 2005-06

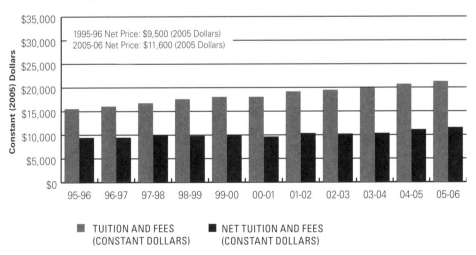

Figure 14:

Full-Time Dependent Student Net Tuition and Fees and Net Cost of Attendance (COA) As a Percentage of Family Income, 1992-93 and 2003-04

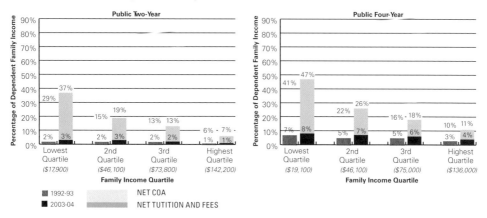

Source: Paying for College: Changes Between 1990 and 2000 for Full-Time Dependent Undergraduates. NCES 2004-075. (National Center for Education Statistics, 2004).

"This is no surprise. We see that the real problem is in the lowest income quartile, and we are all trying to tackle that issue on our campuses. Yet we can also see that a significant percentage of their income is needed for middle-income families to afford college. The question is, do they really have that money, and oftentimes the answer is no."

Donahue outlined the facets of the middle-income dilemma:

- Decline in discretionary income/increase in cost of living
- Social Security and retirement concerns
- Increasing cost of health care/state/local taxes
- Decline in national savings rate
- Erosion of government safety net for middle-income and working poor families
- Job insecurity
- Increasing cost of education

Donahue went on to describe the ramifications for institutions:

- Increasingly expensive to meet "middle-income" need
- Danger of developing a bimodal population of lower- and upper-income students
- Rankings and merit aid
- Issue of "best match"
- Alumni/ae interests

Donahue then shared the story of a fictitious student whose situation is based in the reality of what families and colleges are confronting these days. "I think this dilemma represents what is happening nationwide," Donahue concluded.

Susan Smith, Shrewsbury, Massachusetts

Valedictorian of her high school class, with 2000 on the new SAT, Susan is captain of two varsity sports, and voted most likely to succeed by her classmates. She has been accepted to her dream top private college and the University of Massachusetts (U Mass), and is hoping to pursue a career in sports medicine. Her father (52) has just lost his $85,000/year job as a consultant and her mother (51) is hoping to find a full-time teaching job in the school where she has been a substitute teacher for four years, earning roughly $10,000 a year. Her younger brother, Sherman (14), has a medical condition that requires constant care.

The Smiths bought their modest suburban house in 1985 for $70,000. It is now worth $500,000, and they have been able to consolidate their credit card debts through a recent refinancing of their mortgage so that they now owe $300,000 and pay $2,300 monthly. They have managed to tuck $50,000 into an IRA account, but are not covered by any employer retirement plan; and they will now have to pay $800 monthly for family COBRA health insurance.

Susan Smith's Dilemma

Susan's dream school costs $45,000 and has asked that her parents contribute $15,000. Her financial aid package makes up the difference. After long conversations, the dream school has agreed to increase her grant by $3,000 so that her parents only have to pay $12,000, but this is something they simply cannot afford.

U Mass will cost the family close to the same amount unless she commutes from home, which was not the plan for the Smiths.

Bill Schilling spoke next. "When we discuss middle income, there is little common agreement. I suggest this definition: anyone who is not low income, for whom the issue of college affordability may affect their enrollment decisions. Off the top of my head, that covers incomes of $50,000–$200,000. But there is a lot of variability there, and we have to look at the impact on the family. At the upper end of those ranges, affordability is only an issue at private institutions; a private college may require higher borrowing, lifestyle adjustments, or perhaps going to other than their first-choice college. But most of the people at that income level will certainly be able to afford a four-year public college, or a private college that awards a merit scholarship. From a public policy perspective, these are not significant issues." Schilling shared that Penn provides full financial aid using Institutional Methodology (IM), and has been able to address most of these situations, and the yield is

not significantly less for these families than others. "We have to constantly be sure our need analysis is fair and realistic. We expect families to make some adjustments and make a reasonable contribution."

Schilling continued, "Over the past 5 to 10 years, changes to the College Board IM have made need analysis for middle-income families more reasonable than Federal Methodology. I am particularly concerned about first-generation students from middle-income families. I have seen a shift in IM from assets to income as the primary source of college funds for families. This may be problematic for first-generation families."

Schilling said that if one looks at the lower-income families within the middle-income category, there is a public policy issue. "Some of these families can't afford a four-year public college, given cuts in state funds and increases in tuition. These consequences are more troubling: Student choices are more constrained than those in higher-income brackets." Schilling concluded, "The decisions made about middle-class affordability and access will affect the success of increased lower-income student access. If there is an actual or perceived squeeze on middle-income families, it will be more difficult to gain public and political support to increase lower-income student access."

Tally Hart said, "As I look to the future, I see real jeopardy in the support of education of lower-income students at land-grant institutions, if the middle-income families, who are more numerous, feel so squeezed. The Ohio State University students who are the most needy before institutional aid are the ones who fit the scenario Sally described because they are at the point at or above which support aimed for the lowest income students falls off. A lot of people would say that FM and IM are perhaps too income centered." She stated that she knows families like the Smiths, and probably all in the audience do, as well; they are friends. "One of the most frequent dilemmas our students face is that their parents are willing to borrow, but then do not pass the PLUS credit check."

Over the past five years, tuition has increased by $1,300 at OSU, and state subsidies are down $1,600 per student. They are trying hard to level the field given these shifting resources. The net outcome is a greater demand for institutional financial aid. Hart concluded, "My perfect storm is the really deep conflict between our goals to improve educational opportunities for the lowest income families and the growing pressure on middle-income families and the complexity of what they face."

Stuart Oremus spoke next. "I have heard countless stories about this dilemma from families at my school, in detail and over a number of years. The stories are varied, but the themes are similar, and students are often the ones caught in the middle. They don't want to place an undue burden on their families, or at least are hesitant or embarrassed or confused about financial aid negotiations. When students have been admitted to colleges and the packages are compared, often the dream school is not the one at which the student is allowed to enroll." Oremus said that she tries to work with parents about what they are feeling, and to focus on the best match. She encouraged the participants to "have more dialogue with

The Perfect Storm: The Financial Dilemma Facing Middle-Income
Families Accessing Higher Education

college counselors on this topic, because we have been hearing each individual story for a longer period of time than financial aid officers have."

Don Honeman said, "In some ways, the University of Vermont is the poster child for the privatization of public education. Only 8 percent of our support comes from the state; only 25 percent of our students come from Vermont. I want to address the issue of the middle-income dilemma from an institutional perspective. One of the reasons this has always been a dilemma is that it gets to our institutional priorities. There are not many of us in this room who recognize ourselves as champions for the middle class in terms of what our institutional objectives are. We are champions of low-income students, wanting to provide access for them; we won't admit it, but we are also champions of the wealthy because we recognize the profound impact their revenues have on our fiscal situations. So the middle class is really in the middle; we even pit them against the other two groups. It is not surprising that it lingers as an issue for institutions. As a result of not being championed, the middle class has actually resented some of the goals and aspirations we have for low-income students. I hope we can explore some solutions to this."

Joellen Silberman followed up with a description of the Kalamazoo Promise. Seven anonymous donors have established a program for students who have been enrolled in one of the two Kalamazoo city high schools to receive a scholarship to a Michigan public college upon high school graduation. The amount of the scholarship is prorated based on the number of years of attendance in the city schools; if a student has attended city schools all 12 years, his or her college education is free.

"The initial reaction was to focus on this as a way to bring white middle-income families back into the central city school district from the surrounding suburbs. It was a long time before it was publicized as a promise for kids to go to college who otherwise would not have been able to go. It was more about how middle-income students could go to the University of Michigan instead of Western Michigan University, and not about making college an option for low-income students, and the responsibility of getting them prepared for college."

Heather McDonnell said, "The middle-income group is in eight times more debt than any other income group. They have already made choices that preclude borrowing for college. When I deal with middle-income families, I see, regrettably, two different behaviors. The lower-middle-income group will do whatever it takes to afford a college education. The upper-middle-income families I call the 'T.J. Maxx' group: They want designer experiences for less. This behavior affects college choice. The sticker price keeps them from considering certain schools. I am also very concerned about the schizophrenia within financial aid, that we care about both lower- and middle-income groups."

Silberman added, "There is another band within that middle-income group who are only willing to pay based on the perceived prestige of an institution, or how well it is known."

Honeman cautioned, "'Middle income' is not just about income; it is about values. We have Vermont students from families earning $50,000–$70,000 a year who come to us better

prepared financially than wealthier families from suburban Boston. Choices have been made by parents, and we can't solve that problem for them."

Silberman said, "Culturally, there is very little focus, in terms of major purchases, on the long term. Young people are less interested in saving for a down payment; they want to figure out how to borrow the down payment so that they can have the house now. We as a society have encouraged this type of behavior."

McDonnell added, "We haven't done a good job as financial aid officers of explaining that it is not just current assets and income that parents need to think about in terms of affording college: It is the range of choices and investments they make over a long period of time."

The audience then had a chance to respond. Cathy Thomas, associate dean and director of enrollment services and financial aid at the University of Southern California, said, "We held out the promise to families over time: that college would be there for them if they worked hard—and now middle-income families can't afford the cost. We owe something to these people who we promised we would be able to enroll."

Lynn Nichelson, director of financial aid at Illinois Wesleyan University, spoke about a related issue. "I haven't heard much about gapping. Many colleges can't afford to meet full need. We have serious concerns about it; it relates to alternative loans. We track the loans our students take out because we know over the longer term it affects the alumni giving rate, the institutional default rate, and other issues. We have also learned that if you want to retain lower-income students, institutions need to offer grants. The ability to borrow is what is left to the middle class."

Wendy Beckemeyer said, "When I worked at Colby-Sawyer, if parents did not qualify for PLUS loans, they would begin to look at alternative loans. We would talk with those families and say that it was not the right time for the student to come because it didn't make any sense for them financially. Many of them would come to us two years later, having saved money at a two-year college; in the long run they were more successful both educationally and financially."

Clint Gassaway, director of financial aid at Wabash College, said, "One thing we need to do in concert with admissions and aid officers and guidance counselors is talk much sooner with families. We need to help the middle class make better financial decisions."

McDonnell added, "We need to be more honest about affordability for parents *and* for colleges. Can a college afford to support certain families for four years?"

Honeman followed up, "Admissions and aid do overlap in responsibility. We need to provide better full disclosure. We need to share with students the sobering choices ahead; students shouldn't take on huge debt and expect to pay it off easily over the next 20 years. We have heard some sobering information about their future."

Hart said, "There has been an unraveling of the understanding of college costs. Parents look at the total cost of private schools but, somehow, when they look at public schools, they look at tuition only and then are surprised by room and board and other costs. If students choose to or have to commute, they lose out on the developmentally appropriate experience. We need to do a better job of defining and communicating costs."

Laura Talbot, director of financial aid at Swarthmore College, stated, "Our board of trustees is very concerned with the middle-class dilemma. But they can't describe or define or really understand what the middle class is."

Marc Camille, dean of admission at Xavier University, said, "When I think about the environment today for families, we have a responsibility to change our counseling about affording college. We need to talk about affordability over four years so our families can make more informed decisions."

Michael Mills, associate provost of university enrollment at Northwestern University, spoke about breaks the middle class does have, such as the Hope tax credit or tuition deductibility, which are targeted at middle-income families. "If you run the numbers, if you make $75,000 to $150,000, that places you in the 28 percent tax bracket, squarely in the middle-income category. Over four years, credits save $12,000 in actual tax money. We have been too cautious in terms of talking people through these options. They are underutilized. Fifty percent of the families who claimed but did not get the whole benefit had their taxes done by professional tax preparers. It is a gigantic benefit."

Honeman added, "I agree that we can do a better job of counseling students and families; we can do a better job of advocating for a more reasonable balance between merit and need-based aid on the campus; we can advocate for public policy that focuses on better sensitivity to needs. But at the end of the day, the only really practical thing we can do as a profession is to take the needs analysis system more seriously so that we can ensure a fairer distribution of limited funding for middle-class students. We can't ignore the inequities built into the Federal Methodology. I think we can do this successfully at the professional level."

Jim Belvin, director of financial aid at Duke University, said, "I think the education community fails families. Many families say they were told that, if their student was admitted, they could afford it. We don't help families prepare for what really faces them. We fail them at middle school, not talking about what will be necessary to be prepared financially. We fail them at the time they enroll by not preparing them for the realities they face. We need to explain those realities better: Paying for college is hard and families will have to make some sacrifices. Whatever we are able to offer in terms of aid, short of getting a full ride, paying for college will take sacrifices."

Joe Paul Case, dean and director of financial aid at Amherst College, said, "One of the questions we've begged is the fairness of the system, other than what Don just mentioned. Parental contribution is what we define it to be; it hasn't been adequately revisited. The 'pinch factor' is the percentage of family income required at the cusp. We should rethink need analysis in light of that pinch."

Removing Barriers to College Access and Success for Students from Low-Income Backgrounds

Steve Brooks, executive director of the North Carolina State Education Assistance Authority, and Youlonda Copeland-Morgan, vice president and dean of admission and financial aid at Harvey Mudd College, and Trustee of the College Board, shared information about the College Board Task Force on College Access for Students from Low-Income Backgrounds. An initiative of the College Board Trustees, the task force's purpose is "to forge a collaborative agreement between the Board and its members that will create a commonly accepted definition of 'low-income' and to seek to remove ALL identifiable barriers, including the very important but often overlooked nonfinancial barriers, to college access for those who meet that definition."

Brooks led off by showing the first version of a video that is being developed to use at upcoming College Board regional meetings. Then he gave a brief history of the task force, beginning with ideas that were expressed during and after a Trustees meeting in January 2005. The Financial Aid Standards and Services Advisory Committee (FASSAC) endorsed the idea of setting up a task force to address the barriers facing students from low-income families, and then the Trustees adopted the proposal, "unanimously and enthusiastically," in March 2005.

Members of the task force were chosen to provide a wide perspective based on their current and previous experience in dealing with theses issues. Members, in addition to Steve Brooks and Youlonda Copeland-Morgan, are:

- Dorothy Sexton, vice president for governance and secretary, The College Board
- J. David Armstrong, Jr., chancellor, Florida Community Colleges and Workforce Education
- William D. Boyd, associate vice president of student services and budget administration, San Diego State University
- Jacquelyn M. Belcher, former president, Georgia Perimeter Community College
- Linda M. Clement, vice president for student affairs, University of Maryland at College Park
- George Chin, director of student financial assistance, City University of New York
- Ann S. Coles, senior vice president of College Access Programs, The Education Resources Institute
- Carroll K. Davis, coordinator for college counseling, North Central High School (IN)

Removing Barriers to College Access and Success for Students from Low-Income Backgrounds

- Georgette DeVeres, associate vice president of admission and financial aid, Claremont McKenna College
- Pamela Fowler, director of financial aid, University of Michigan at Ann Arbor
- Joel V. Harrell, higher education consultant
- Kathleen Little, senior executive director of financial aid services, The College Board
- Jerome A. Lucido, vice provost for enrollment policy and management, University of North Carolina at Chapel Hill
- Patricia Martin, assistant vice president of the National Office for School Counselor Advocacy, The College Board
- Ronald S. Martinez, director of financial aid, University of New Mexico at Albuquerque
- William Schilling, director of student financial aid, University of Pennsylvania
- Laurice "Penny" Sommers, coordinator for Los Angeles Unified School District's High School Programs
- Shirley Ort, associate provost and director of scholarships and student aid, University of North Carolina at Chapel Hill, and chair-elect, College Scholarship Assembly
- Ann Wright, vice president of the Southwest Region, The College Board

Brooks added, "In addition to the insights of our task force members, we have received tremendous interest and feedback from the membership of the organization as a whole. And we are looking to work with more and more students and more and more counselors as we go along."

Brooks went on to describe the two phases of the effort:

- Phase 1: Better define the issue, pinpoint relevant research, and propose possible solutions.
- Phase 2: Recruit a second group of leaders who will collaborate with the College Board in removing barriers to higher education and who can assist in promoting the work of the task force, resulting in buy-in from nonmember institutions, outreach programs, and policymakers.

Brooks indicated that Phase 1 is what the current task force is doing; Phase 2 will include perhaps some of those people but many others in the public policy sector as well.

In terms of Phase 1, he shared that defining the target group is a complex process: "They are an elusive concept. Once we agree on some definition, we want to target a variety of efforts to streamline processes and eliminate barriers. I think that we have discovered that there will be multiple definitions and multiple solutions—but we hope to come up with a commonly accepted set of definitions and solutions. The focus in phase 1 will be on solutions that are practical.

Copeland-Morgan then spoke. "This task is a daunting one, but one that is very appropriate for the College Board to take on; it is an area where we have not made significant progress as a country." She gave an overview of what the task force has accomplished in its three meetings to date:.

- Defined the role of the task force
- Decided the depth and breadth of the undertaking
- Discussed timetables for accomplishing the work
- Brainstormed barriers to access
- Discussed ways to engage the membership
    - National Forum
    - Through the three Assemblies
    - Regional meetings
    - Financial Aid Standards and Services Advisory Committee (FASSAC)
    - Board of Trustees
    - Seek feedback and provide updates via e-mail
- Discussed the importance of developing partnerships with other organizations and associations and possible strategies to achieve this
- Discussed ways in which the task force's work could inform the advocacy agenda of the College Board
- Began communications with membership
    - Held session at National Forum and introduced work of the task force at annual meetings of all Assemblies
    - Will hold sessions at 2006 regional meetings
- Call to membership sent in October notifying the members of the creation of the task force and asking for best practices and research in this area
- Interviews and articles written on the work of the task force
- Currently developing focus groups with high school counselors across the country
- Discussing ways of talking to students, parents, and others

Copeland-Morgan described how brainstorming about the barriers students from low-income backgrounds face in accessing higher education led to the definition of three areas among which those barriers can be divided:

- Preparation
- Admissions and financial aid
- Retention and success

Removing Barriers to College Access and Success for Students
from Low-Income Backgrounds

"Subcommittees of the task force were formed to further flesh out the barriers in each area, identify relevant research on related topics, engage other College Board members in finding possible solutions, and make recommendations that will eliminate barriers and identify best practices within higher education. Ann Coles chairs the preparation subcommittee; Carroll Davis heads the admissions and financial aid subcommittee; and Shirley Ort leads the retention and success subcommittee.

"Students from low-income families face barriers at every stage of the college process. Because we are not using a common definition, students are getting into some programs that help prepare them for college, but then hit the next hurdle." Copeland-Morgan stated that one of the ideas already being discussed at the task force is an "E-ZPass" for students once they have been identified, that would allow them free services and access to PSAT/NMSQT, SAT, and college-prep programs, as well as eligibility for college application fee waivers.

The task force has worked to identify the target groups for their efforts. Copeland-Morgan shared these lists of identifying characteristics that are being considered:

School-Related Factors:

- Traditional college age
- Have participated in free or reduced-lunch program
- Qualify for PSAT/NMSQT or SAT fee waiver
- Attend a Title I school
- Number of emergency-credentialed teachers in the schools
- No requests made for a transcript by March/April of senior year
- Pipeline rates: percentage in high school going on to college; college-going rate of ninth-graders at their high school
- High school's dropout rate
- Percentage of students in high school completing Algebra II
- Low-performing school districts
- No SAT or ACT scores on file

Family-Related Factors:

- Neither parent is a college graduate
- Live in public housing
- Family has never owned a home
- Lack of own transportation
- English not primary language at home
- Homeless

- Foster child
- Parents missing, in jail
- Eligible for food stamps/TANF
- Low socioeconomic status
- Meet federal poverty standard
- No health insurance
- Undocumented/underdocumented
- Zip code
- Number of address changes in first three years of high school
- No banking relationship
- Parents working more than one job
- Number of jobs student is working
- Emancipated high school student
- Student has dependents

In conclusion, Copeland-Morgan related the challenges that face the effort to remove barriers. First is defining what is meant by low-income students. "There is no national standard. As we have discussed the issue as a group, we have reached a consensus that we are not simply talking about an economic situation. For example, should we consider other factors, such as first-generation students? And how would we identify and track these students? We are also looking into which College Board programs and services the identified students should have access to.

"We want to create a national standard so that identified students can have consistent access to programs and services through the entire pipeline to access higher education. This is where Phase 2 will kick in." Services available at the K–12 level might include:

- Outreach programs
- College Board programs and services
- Institutional programs and services
    - Automatically waive the admissions application and deposit fee for these students
    - Provide book store vouchers
    - Provide automatic fee waivers for PSAT/NMSQT, SAT, and CSS/Financial Aid PROFILE®

Removing Barriers to College Access and Success for Students from Low-Income Backgrounds

The audience then had a chance to respond. Daniel Goyette said, "There are already many programs addressing this group of students, both public and private, at the state level, and on individual campuses. What will the connection be to those programs?" Brooks responded, "We are aware of a number of successful programs; this is one of the wonderful insights Ann Coles provides. There is indeed a great variety in these programs. We will focus on developing broad programs, but we are learning from great local ones."

Jack Kopnisky, chief executive officer and president of First Marblehead Corporation, asked how success would be measured. Copeland-Morgan responded, "This is a challenge. We know we need measurement. That will come in part from membership feedback, which we can use to develop a College Board database. If we can provide consistent access to these programs, that would be a success. Once we have defined the target groups and the programs that will reduce barriers for them, we can build in the measurement component." Brooks added, "Even if we only do the E-ZPass from grades 7–12, that will be a success."

Cathy Thomas said she was pleased to see the three subgroups, and that the task force is interested in success as well as access. She believes that one-on-one interaction is critical for these students. "We had 25 Los Angeles students at the University of Southern California this summer; they had been admitted to the top institutions in the country and were entering those campuses in the fall. I did a session on financial literacy and discovered that half the group, in July, did not have their financial aid awards completed. They did what they could on their own, but what their parents needed to do didn't get done. The task force should think about ways to address that issue, as well."

Nancy Meislahn, dean of admission and financial aid at Wesleyan University, said, "We face—and need to deal with—political realities. Many of us as educators are not inclined to be politically active. I hope the task force is thinking about where this fits in the current political reality, what we can do as an organization, and how we can make a call for action that happens at the grassroots level."

Gerard Rooney, vice president of enrollment management and external relations at St. John Fisher College, said, "I would support the involvement of parents as well, especially parents of first-generation college applicants and students."

Bruce Poch, vice president and dean of admissions at Pomona College, said, "I am glad to see progress on this issue, especially the E-ZPass concept. But I am concerned that it might take too much time to get results. We should be able to reach these students through Student Search—we should be able to select on income. Also, the structure of the PROFILE fees should be changed; colleges ought to pay a flat fee based on the number of students who enroll. Finally, we need to include on the task force some counselors who can provide an 'on the ground' perspective."

Jerry Lucido responded as a member of the task force. "Making income a Student Search selector is an active issue before the Guidance and Admission Assembly Council. As for how to work together, the Board can bring us together and energize us as a task force, but we have to be the troops on the ground. This feedback mechanism is terribly important. We struggle with what the task force can do and what then the individual institutions have to do."

Judy Lewis Logue said, "I am grateful for the task force, as this issue has been neglected for 15 years. But you will need to be a catalyst for individual colleges because economic diversity is not as valued on the college side as it should be."

Copeland-Morgan concluded, "Well, this gives you an idea of how our discussions have gone. We appreciate the ideas you have shared. I would ask you to look beyond the current titles of the task force members: They have played a variety of professional roles and have a wealth of experience. Many of them have high school experience, and we are talking with counselors in focus groups, so this perspective is actively involved.

"We encourage you to continue to provide us with feedback. We can't solve the whole problem—but I am confident that, when this project is completed, all of us will be able to do a better job of providing access for those from low-income backgrounds."

What Americans Think About the Value of Education and Its Relationship to Success

Peter Hart, chief executive officer of Peter D. Hart Research Associates, gave a lively presentation of recent research into how Americans view education. "I want to start with some impressions of where we are as a society. More than anything else, when the public talks about what is responsible for our success as a nation, they say it's our education system. That's truly a remarkable insight into the American public: Education is more important than democracy, our entrepreneurial culture, military strength, or natural resources."

Figure 17: Public Education Responsible for America's Success

Which of these factors is most responsible for America's success in the world?

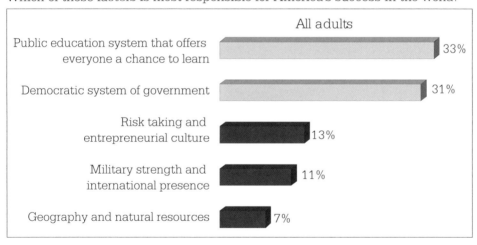

Source: *Education and Its Relationship to Success*, Peter D. Hart

"In fact, 85 percent of the public says education is essential or important for getting ahead. Every time a governor has made an outstanding contribution to the education system, the public puts him or her on a pedestal.

"One of the questions we have been asking is what the public is thinking in terms of the future. We have always thought of ourselves as handing the baton forward; that things are going to be better for our kids than they were for us. But now there is fear and uncertainty. Younger people are still optimistic but, in general, the public is concerned.

"And we are uncertain as to whether we will be a world leader in education in 20 to 30 years. This is scary, because we believe education is where we get our success as a nation."

Figure 18: Will U.S. Be a World Leader in Education in 20–30 Years?

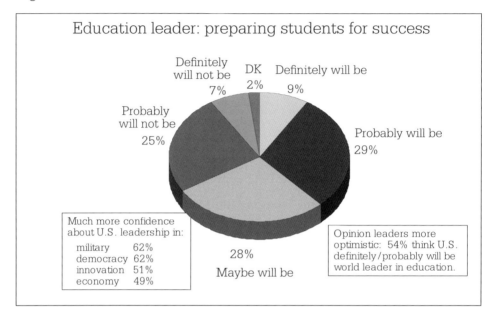

Source: Education and Its Relationship to Success, Peter D. Hart

Hart then described research that his company will be releasing soon about the best strategy for competing in a global society. "We gave the public a choice: When it comes to competing, should the United States focus on getting smarter or being tougher?" They polled 250 opinion elites as well as the general public. "The public by a slight plurality says we need to get tougher." Hart noted the differences of opinion by groups based on education, job type, age, and Hispanic background. "Opinion leaders know what the issues are, but leadership is needed. We need to break through, in part, on the immigration issue. We need to think of all the advancements we have had in terms of attracting foreign-born students who have stayed here. Now, we are educating foreign students who go back to their countries. We won't be the beneficiary; we will lose these people."

Hart then described research methods used for the information he would be presenting next from an ETS study. In April 2005, his firm surveyed 2,250 adults nationwide, including 1,009 members of the general public and 66 parents of K–12 students, of whom 371 were parents of high school students. They did an additional 300 interviews among adults in California, Ohio, and New Jersey, with high school administrators, and among high school teachers. They also held four focus groups; at each location, one group was composed of high school administrators and the other was composed of parents of high school students.

In general, parents feel that educational quality has dropped.

As for No Child Left Behind, most have heard of it. "But the problem is, no one has seen reform. The branding is way ahead of the product. The product isn't known, and for those who do know more about it, they tend to be least favorable about the program. The gap between parents and teachers as to the value of NCLB is significant.

Figure 19: Grades for Nation's Schools Remain at "C"

	All adults					Parents		
	2005	2004	2003	2002	2001	2005	2004	2001
A	3%	2%	2%	2%	2%	4%	2%	8%
B	23%	20%	29%	14%	18%	27%	20%	**35%**
C	46%	**47%**	**47%**	**50%**	**51%**	46%	**48%**	**33%**
D	15%	15%	13%	21%	16%	12%	14%	13%
F	4%	4%	2%	4%	3%	2%	3%	4%
GPA	2.1	2.0	2.2	1.9	2.0	2.2	2.0	2.3

Spring 2005

The Public's Report Card
The Nation's Schools

Source: Education and Its Relationship to Success, Peter D. Hart

"A majority of adults feel that high school needs to change. Elementary is the priority for parents, but high school needs changes, too."

Figure 20: Majority Believe High Schools Need Major Change

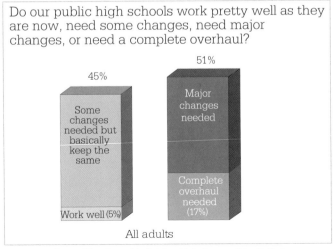

Do our public high schools work pretty well as they are now, need some changes, need major changes, or need a complete overhaul?

45% — Some changes needed but basically keep the same
51% — Major changes needed
Work well (5%)
Complete overhaul needed (17%)

All adults

Source: Education and Its Relationship to Success, Peter D. Hart

"There are three important lessons that come from this. First, the schools aren't doing well. Second, this reform is known and it has not gained traction. It needs to gain a lot more respect from teachers and parents alike. And third, in the end, we don't have a strategy on how to approach it. Political and educational leaders have not provided that sense of insight."

Hart continued, "Education is both a partisan and a bipartisan issue: bipartisan from the fact that the public just wants the education system to improve, but partisan because when you ask the public which party would be best in dealing with education issues, the Democrats have a nearly 20-point advantage. After the environment, Social Security, and health care, this is the best issue for Democrats."

The public is not sure how it wants accountability judged. "They do want the bar to be raised. They want accountability."

Hart described "the second disconnect" as the different views parents and teachers have of the purpose of high school. Parents want students to better themselves with a tangible goal; teachers want to develop literate, educated citizens. Parents are practical; teachers are idealistic.

Figure 21: Different Views on Purpose of High Schools

Single top goal of a high school education

	HS parents	HS teachers
Prepare youth to continue education in college, technical, trade school	41%	19%
Produce literate, educated citizens who participate in democracy	19%	35%
Teach students to think	17%	23%
Prepare good workers who can succeed in modern economy	9%	14%
Teach students about building strong character	8%	2%
Teach basics in reading, writing, math	4%	3%

Source: Education and Its Relationship to Success, Peter D. Hart

The public thinks the main problem high schools have is that they have to deal with problems inside and outside of high school.

"The question then becomes, where do we focus? We remain what I would consider a middle-class society. We are constantly concerned about 'what does it mean to the middle?'. Should our challenge be to get the best people as far up the ladder as possible, or to help those people who are down at the bottom to move up, or is it the middle we should focus

on? Most of the public are more interested in the middle group." Hart said a more detailed breakdown indicated that those who believed we should focus on the bottom included 25 percent of blue-collar workers, 35 percent of African Americans, 29 percent of Hispanics, and 18 percent of whites.

Hart then shared proposals that the survey presented to those being polled. Each of the proposals received support from 70 to 90 percent of the people polled; the following data reflects only those who said they strongly favored each proposal. The results show that people especially want qualified teachers and they want education to be practical, with internship and work-study experiences.

"Should you feel supported as educators? Yes, you have public support. But the public is hungry for reform. They believe in education, and they see us getting behind. They believe we have to do something. They want to raise the bar on education, but be sure that it is practical. They see teachers at the heart of education."

Figure 22: All Proposals Receive Support

% who strongly favor each	
Ensure teachers expert in subject: certification test	74%
Emphasize real-world learning: work-study, community service, vocational courses	64%
Transform senior year: work-study, industry cert/job training, college classes	57%
Statewide test on mastery of core subjects to graduate	53%
Raise teacher salaries to hire/retain good teachers even if taxes increase	51%

Source: Education and Its Relationship to Success, Peter D. Hart

The public says it would support increased funding, even if it increased taxes. "This always tests much better than the reality. Increased school funding is often voted down because people do not trust that improvement will happen and that their money will be well spent. If you are going to 'sell' education costs, you need to be able to clearly exhibit fiscal discipline and accountability."

The public knows that if we do not do something about the status quo, we are going to go downhill.

Hart concluded the presentation with some suggestions:

- **Talk to the public about raising the bar.** They want that. Give them a horizon of where we need to go.
- **Use global competition as a factor.** The public thinks that China is going to pass us. That can be used as a leverage point. At the heart of this is our education system; if we don't get that right, nothing else is going to be right.
- **Be creative.** Develop the ability to explain the new ideas. Put reform into a package that they understand, that sounds like it will work, and that is practical.
- **Be rigorous.** In terms of testing, or financial discipline, or anything else. People want accountability.
- **Provide a set of measuring rods so the public knows where we are going.** We need to give a starting point, show progress and end goals.

"The public is exceptionally pragmatic. They want to invest, but they want to invest in what will work. When it comes to education, we are not ideologues. People can work together on this issue."

The audience then had a chance to respond. Richard Shaw said, "We are an aging country. Often communities that are aging seem to vote against school bonds. Do people become less supportive of education as they age, and how does the concern they feel about health care affordability fit in?" Hart replied, "Elderly people vote overwhelmingly against school bonds. In part it is because it is not their issue but, more importantly, it is not their children's issue. Their children are out of school and their grandchildren are going to school elsewhere. Against that, I think the baby boomers will be more supportive as they get older because they see education as having been crucial to their success and they are becoming the most affluent group in our society. And a lot of them are or will be going back to school. At the same time, it is always going to be hard to get seniors invested in education spending. As for health care, we just *have* to solve the problem. It is the practical element of life; we need to make the case for education as the aspirational element and the competitive element."

Michael Behnke asked Hart to comment on the concept that schools in general need improvement, but their own schools are fine. "Is this a combination of racism and of suburban and gated community antipathy toward urban school systems?" Hart responded, "You are exactly right. Our evaluation of the school system as a whole is based upon how we perceive inner-city schools. In part, it is because that is where the major publicity comes from. In terms of looking at their own schools, by and large the numbers are pretty good. Even urban parents rate their school systems as far better than the system as a whole. But if you compare how African Americans and Caucasians feel about their schools, there is a 15-point gap, and with Hispanics, an eight- to nine-point gap."

Matthew Fissinger, director of admission at Loyola Marymount University, asked, "Did your work touch on perceptions of affordability? Is the problem about support based on

the perceived overwhelming amounts of money families need to pay for college or on the communities' need to fix the schools?" Hart said, "I have looked at it in the past. On the affordability issue, parents say they get a better 'education buy' by sending their students to a two-year college first, and then to a state college or university. This gets back to the need for institutions to show that they are doing their best with their dollars, that they are financially rigorous."

Wrap-Up

James Montoya, vice president of higher education assessments, services, and regions at the College Board, gave an insightful wrap-up to the Colloquium. "Gary Orfield painted a frightening picture. But he also helped us understand our role in being part of the system that encourages stratification and exclusion, particularly at a time when human capital is an incredibly valuable resource in a postindustrial society. And he also introduced the concept of a collective voice and of a collective will. He reminded us that in 1976-77 the college-going rate among racial and ethnic groups showed no gap. There was a time in higher education history when we had the will and the resources to tackle what at that time seemed an impossible task. He also reminded us that we cannot deal with the current situation institution by institution, but we need a collective voice, and organizations and associations willing to take a leadership role."

Montoya said partnerships were the key to success in the late 1970s, especially the partnership between the federal government and higher education, which began to erode in the 1980s, when education began to be seen as a private and not a public good. He remarked that during the Colloquium, the participants saw examples of partnerships that work: the College Board and Florida; the partnership between two-year, four-year, and K–12; higher education and organizations like Posse; higher education and the corporate sector; financial aid and offices of international education; admissions officers, financial aid officers, and faculty working together; and the College Board Task Force on College Access for Students from Low-Income Backgrounds working with other organizations and members.

"The two partnerships that were very key to me were the partnership between admissions and financial aid and the faculty at an institution, and the partnership between higher education and the corporate sector. The intersection, in some ways, came at a peculiar place for me, and that was with Professor Johnson's concept of intellectual entrepreneurship, 'the transformation of universities,' as he put it, 'into entrepreneurially oriented economic engines.'" While Montoya was at first uncomfortable with the idea of higher education as an economic engine, he was able to put together a faculty–corporate partnership concept.

"For example, Professors Covarrubias and Katanski used certain words that suggested what the corporate sector is suggesting: that, as institutions, we need to be more nimble, move more rapidly, and prepare interculturalists. We need to rethink our notions of borders and barriers. We need to take advantage of the transition and transformation of the faculty. Forty-four percent of our faculty are part-time. As Dr. Johnson said, we will see a major transformation. How will we take advantage of that in order to create the global citizens that we need?

"The concept from Professor Covarrubias that we need to reconfigure the system, rather than reconfigure the students, is not that foreign from the corporate sector's model of how we need to reconfigure our institutions. We need to build a business case and, as Peter Hart just reminded us, we need to be accountable." Montoya added that global competitiveness, a topic throughout the Colloquium, is something to which we need to give much more thought, since we will need to prepare our students for a global economy.

"It is also clear that we need to educate the corporate sector and the public to help them better understand the role of education. They understand the importance, but communication between faculty, institutions, and the public is only going to become more important. We have to find common ground language that allows us to converge our visions and move forward together."

Montoya listed other words that he will take away:

• Engagement

• Purpose

• Energy

• Grit and traction

• Progress

• Collaborative work

• Creativity

He believes that the new model for success at Kalamazoo is not only very appropriate to their mission, but also applicable to all of us as educators.

"I am walking out of here thinking about that very simple notion, of the necessity of identifying those people with a twinkle in their eye. It is our responsibility to leave this Colloquium with a twinkle in our eye. Though we have discussed desperation, we have also seen hope from some of the best practices that have been discussed. We know that inspiration springs from desperation or from hope. We have seen both, and been inspired by both. I hope that I am sending you off inspired to be part of that collective voice, to be part of the collective will, and to do what we can to work institutionally but, most importantly, collectively to try to make progress on this most important endeavor.

"Thank you for your time and energy, your ideas, and your voices."

Appendix A
Betraying the American Dream and Closing the College Gate
Keynote Address by Gary Orfield

We are going through a huge transformation in our society; it is the last generation of a European–American majority in our population and the first in the globalized postindustrial economy where education is the key to individual and national success. Unfortunately, we're going through it in a period of weak leadership with very limited vision, and the result is a major threat to our future. Without intending to, we are building a very deep social and economic crisis for our country. As our country is being transformed, we are reversing policies that were very positive, if perhaps too limited, responses in favor of policies that increase inequality. It is easy to blame the political leaders, who deserve strong criticism, but it is much harder to face the fact that our own limited responses on campus are often obscuring and sometimes compounding the problems. Higher education can do better.

The increasing racial and ethnic diversity of the country brings challenges to all of us, not to just figure out what we do in our own institution, but how we can act as a community to create an awareness of what we need to do collectively. It is not about small local policies, though those matter. The future shape of society is at stake. In 2003, 58 percent of the children in American public schools were white, 17 percent African American, and 19 percent Latino. But just 8.8 percent of the B.A. degrees in the country went to African Americans and 6.3 percent to Latinos. Doctoral degree numbers are much worse, suggesting huge faculty problems in the future. These results are not compatible with a viable national future for a nation that will have a large nonwhite majority.

The extent of the racial transformation of America is not as clear in higher education as it is in elementary and secondary education since many nonwhite students disappear on the path to college, and many who enroll leave after a short time. By 2004, the public schools of the West were 53 percent nonwhite and those of the South 50 percent nonwhite, and both regions were facing ongoing changes. The U.S. Census projects that in the middle of the century we're going to have a population of only about 40 percent white school-age children. Yet, in every part of the country, schools are becoming more segregated as minority populations grow, and desegregation efforts are shut down by conservative courts. The vast majority of these segregated schools have concentrated poverty and many have linguistic segregation as well, a damaging triple segregation. They have less competitive peer groups, less experienced and qualified teachers, more disruption, fewer honors and AP courses, and many forms of inequality. These are the schools that are being judged as failures by No Child Left Behind. Our book, *Dropouts in America: Confronting the Graduation Rate Crisis* (Harvard Education Press) shows that in the typical high-poverty minority high school less than half the kids are graduating; and few finish with the tools you need in college. Too often we adopt policies that treat students as if they have had equal opportunity in high school, which is absurd and unfair.

In the face of this challenge, we are forgetting the promises we made in more generous times. After World War II we had a gigantic expansion of educational opportunity in this country. One of the very best investments any country has ever made in its future was the GI Bill, which broke the link between family income and college for veterans. In the 1960s, we had an explosion of higher education opportunities. Community colleges sprouted everywhere; teacher's colleges became state universities; research universities multiplied. In 1965, the Higher Education Act provided federal aid for poor children to go to college, and the Poverty Program created programs to recruit and prepare them. At the peak of the civil rights revolution, in 1964, Congress passed the first major Civil Rights Act in almost 100 years, which made it illegal to discriminate in any institution that received federal aid in education. The result of those changes was a society much more equitable in terms of access to higher education. College tuitions in public institutions were low. With a good summer job, many students could earn enough money to go to a public university if they lived at home. Anybody with a high school degree had the right to go to a four-year college in many states. With the Pell Grant in the early 1970s, with low tuition, with the huge expansion of spaces for higher education, and with the Civil Rights Act, we promised to make college available as we made high school available earlier. In this period of higher education expansion, we had a level of higher education that exceeded almost every place else in the world.

However, things turned back in the 1980s as we began a period still continuing to raise our tuitions much faster than family incomes were going up, increasingly shifting aid to the middle class, and cutting back state support. Beginning in the early 1980s, almost all of our states adopted the so-called high-tuition and high-aid theory but then failed to provide sufficient aid, increasingly excluding lower-income students. We've transferred aid from the poor to the middle class since the Middle-Income Student Assistance Act in 1978. The loan provision was made a right, but Pell Grants always depended on annual appropriations, which have covered less and less of college costs since the Reagan cutbacks. Of course, the Clinton administration accelerated this process when it created the tax expenditures in the repayment of student loans, something that doesn't do anything for creating access for poor kids who cannot pay first and get the subsidy later. As education has become more important we've fallen behind in college access, especially for the rapidly growing Latino and black communities. The Organizations for Economic Co-operation and Development reports that we're behind New Zealand, Finland, Sweden, Poland, Norway, Netherlands, Korea, and several others. We've slipped way behind in terms of real access to higher education.

A serious retreat in civil rights began in the Reagan administration, which gutted the effort to enforce the higher education desegregation standards in the 19 states that had unconstitutionally created racially separate higher education institutions. Conservatives began an attack on affirmative action, which has now been outlawed in four states and has survived nationally by the vote of a single justice in the hard-fought 2003 University of

Michigan case. Right now the Bush administration is threatening some institutions that are trying to maintain minority-access programs with their attack on Southern Illinois University and other places, misusing the power granted by the Civil Rights Act, and with the confirmation of two new Supreme Court justices who have a history of opposition to affirmative action.

As the demand for college surpasses the creation of new spaces, we have an increasing reliance on tests for admissions, reducing open-access, four-year institutions and increasing the stratification of students between community colleges and four-year colleges under the false assumption that this produces fair access. Most states are cutting back on remediation in their four-year institutions, ignoring the inferior preparation that minority students get in high school and pretending, in spite of decades of evidence, that this can be solved by high-stakes exit exams.

Since the 1970s, black college-going rates increased. Latinos, however, show little real change over the 30-year period. The completion statistics are a much worse story than the access numbers. Too many students enroll, take out loans, and get nothing.

The effects of educational attainment on family and community income and wealth are huge and growing. White high school dropouts made an average of $19,000 in total income in 2002; high school graduates made about $10,000 more. Some college helped a little. A bachelor's degree makes a big difference. Unfortunately, attainment is very strongly linked to family advantages. Within racial groups, college going reflects social and economic status. In the top quartile, 88 percent went to college from the class of 1992; from the bottom quartile 36 percent. This is a society where mobility is increasingly based on an education, and education is increasingly ossifying its social structure. Especially when you rely too much on things that are very powerfully related to parent income and educational levels and the quality of the high school, such as tests and AP courses for admission, a vicious cycle of intergenerational inequality is fostered.

If we've implicitly redefined access to mean access to a community college, we have to face the reality that all community colleges are not created equal. Students in white suburban community colleges and the poor black and Latino colleges, who have the same goals, have profoundly different probabilities of realizing them. We are giving too many low-income minority students the idea they are going to college like white students even when they go to an institution where almost nobody ever completes and successfully transfers to get a B.A. We have to worry about whether we're reproducing at this level the same type of inequality we see in the high schools of the country. If that's what we're doing, we're becoming a part of the problem, claiming to have a structure offering fair opportunities while running one where too many minority students enter dead ends.

Projecting our population transformation tells us that we're going to have to deal with the racial and economic diversity; otherwise, we won't have students. In the next decade, students of color will increase far more rapidly than whites. Later there will be a decline in the number of whites. Given the segregation of neighborhoods and public schools, college may also be the only place where we can train people to function effectively across the racial and ethnic lines that must be crossed to operate successful institutions and communities in the future.

There is, of course, a dimension of simple self-interest about the future of our economy. If we had an enemy who was going to steal our most important resource and destroy our future, we would be mobilizing with all our energy. Well, our young people—increasingly nonwhite students—are our most important resource, and in a postindustrial society the educational level of the population is the only really important resource that is irreplaceable. It is being threatened, but far from mobilizing we are playing interest group politics and adopting policies that compound the threat. One of the policies that makes the least sense in this context is "merit assistance." Starting with the Georgia Hope Scholarship and going through a number of state programs like Bright Futures in Florida, we've had states that are not funding their higher education systems very well, haven't been expanding capacity adequately, and have not been funding access for low-income students decide to massively fund students who don't show any financial need at all but whose parents are middle- and upper-class suburban voters. This is a policy that is profoundly counterproductive and, of course, very popular with the families who receive this subsidy. What we are doing on a federal level by funding retroactively lower costs through tax credits for students who have already gone to college and have graduated and are paying off their student loans is a similar story. This tax subsidy that has virtually no impact on attendance is now costing more than the entire Pell Grant budget. This is also the direction that many institutions are taking, giving aid to students who do not need it but have high scores in order to look good in the *U.S. News & World Report* ratings and in recruitment.

Higher education leaders cannot be passive about these choices. If we're not providing equity for lower-income and working-class people, providing the possibility of making it into the middle class, can we in good conscience take public funds and shift them to some people who would get it anyway and whose parents have given them tremendous advantages? Over 70 percent of white families own homes and have equity, and they can draw on it but we exclude that as a college resource in the aid formulas. Most minority families have little net worth to draw on. When they get an "unmet need" statement in their children's aid package, it means their children are not going to go to college because they just don't have the resources. We have to be conscious of these things and we have to think about what's it like for families who have never owned anything and have never taken on any debt, who don't have any credit rating or bank relationship, to file very complicated forms and to find a lending institution to relate to and so forth. We have to have a realistic picture of what kind of a society we are and what has to be done to really make access possible.

Costs are going up much faster than income, the burden is being shifted from the state to individual families, family income is becoming increasingly unequal, and the aid that is available is too often being shifted from those who desperately need it to those who have high scores and the resources to pay their own way. So what do we do about this if we're a society that wants to address these issues and turn around this picture? If we follow the existing pattern, we're in danger of having a generation who is going to be less qualified on average than the present generation and less able to produce wealth, with a deep and self-perpetuating racial inequality. We have every probability of shunting very large numbers of people out of a productive economy into a destructive economy or into poverty and dead-end jobs. The trends would increasingly deny the right to go to a four-year college to lower-income or nonwhite students. We need to think about this; we need to have an inter-generation and cross-racial discussion about what is going on and what the consequences are.

We are excluding groups that are going to be the majority. We may create an increasingly polarized society, very hard to govern. We assume we can be increasingly punitive and exclusive and nothing bad will happen. The recent massive demonstrations about immigration show that there are limits to what people will accept. In a world where ethnic polarization is all too frequent and tragic we are foolish to bet that we can safely ignore the profound exclusion of constantly growing numbers of young people.

I think one of the great things about our country is we all have a common dream. It is a dream that we can get an education and a job and afford a home that is decent for our family to live in; that we can send our kids to college and give them a good start. It's not a dream that's different across ethnic and racial lines. If the excluded groups start realizing that it's often a lie and we can't do that anymore, it will be a very major threat to our society. So far, that hasn't happened. So far the dream has been held very deeply and very steadily. It seems to me that everyone in higher education has a responsibility to make that dream real as much as possible and not to allow ourselves to become part of a system of growing stratification and exclusion.

What I think is happening in higher education right now is that year by year, because we don't get enough public dollars, we pass costs onto the students. We think that is the only thing we can do and ignore the cumulating consequences. Otherwise, we have to remove faculty, eliminate programs, or something else. If you make that same calculation year after year for 25 years, which is what we've been doing in quite a few states, eventually you have a different kind of institution and a different system of opportunity. Eventually you have a different type of society. What we do to protect our institutions, individually, by keeping our faculty and programs going and keeping our rankings up and attracting good students, collectively does not work for our society.

We have to have a broader vision, and we have to figure out how to be a community that speaks to the rest of our society. We have to tell all groups that we really do believe in their dreams and we believe they need to be realized. And we need to explain that it is going to be costly, and we're going to have to pay for it because it is the best possible investment.

We're going to have to tax people. We're in a capitalist society where everybody says, you have to pay for what you get, except when it comes to education. We have to enter into that debate. We have to enter into the debate about what is necessary to have a decent society and the fact that we've really gone too far in cutting public resources.

We also have to enter into the debate about relative priorities. Is it more important to put somebody in jail for 60 years because they have had a minor drug offense or to send several more people to college? Is it more important to institute a small tax cut than to keep public universities affordable for the public?

There was a remarkable mobilization of the higher education world to defend affirmative action in the University of Michigan Supreme Court case. People from colleges all across the country reached out and they worked together with leaders in business, with minority communities, with people from the military and many institutions that realized that we really couldn't have a viable society unless we could work across racial and ethnic lines and train the potential leaders from all groups.

That victory was a huge accomplishment, but we have to go beyond the issue of affirmative action, beyond the issue of getting black and Latino and American Indian students admitted to our selective colleges and universities, though that remains a very important issue. We must make it feasible for them to actually enroll and succeed. We must create better high school options to get talented minority and low-income students ready for college. We need strong outreach and transition programs that recruit and identify talent and make up for previous educational deficits. We have to talk about policies that give unfair advantages to those from the most privileged families. We have to recognize that in a society in transformation with a fundamentally unequal education, remediation is an essential investment in fairness and development of all our talent. We have to recognize that if we don't have enough course offerings and counseling in our community colleges, people are going to be losing their eligibility and they're not going to be able to complete any degree. We have to talk about getting enough aid for students so they can actually go to a public four-year institution if they are poor or the working class, and to make that a higher priority than other things that we would like to do, like giving high-scoring students a special scholarship. We have to look at the racial consequences and the social stratification consequences of all of our actions.

This is a society that is in danger of losing its promise, losing its flexibility, losing its mobility, and is creating a generation who is less capable, and we're in a world where the cost of doing that will be huge, making it all but impossible for us to maintain the kind of role we have had in the world. I encourage you to not only think about this in terms of what you can do in your institutions, but also in terms of the kind of public voice you need to have and how we can explain to our officials the costs of continuing on the path that we are going. The promise of the 1960s and 1970s offered a generous vision of true opportunity as well as a shrewd investment in the future that is paying many rewards now. We need to turn back to that path and renew that promise.

Appendix B
List of Participants

2006 Colloquium Participants

Robert Adams Vice President, Student Affairs	Santa Monica College	adams_robert@smc.edu
Diane Anci Dean of Admission	Mount Holyoke College	danci@mtholyoke.edu
David Armstrong Chancellor	Florida Community Colleges and Workforce Education	david.armstrong@fldoe. org
Benedict Baglio Consultant for Guidance Services	Cold Spring Harbor High School	asop@optonline.net
Cindy Bailey Executive Director, Higher Education Solutions	The College Board	cbailey@collegeboard.org
Tim Bailey Director, Education Finance Services	The College Board	tbailey@collegeboard.org
Philip Ballinger Director of Admissions	University of Washington	philipba@u.washington. edu
Mary Lou Bates Dean of Admissions & Financial Aid	Skidmore College	mbates@skidmore.edu
James Bauer Assistant Dean, Enrollment Management and Director, Financial Assistance	University of Miami	jbauer@miami.edu
Wendy Beckemeyer Vice President, Enrollment Management	Alfred University	beckemeyer@alfred.edu
Michael Behnke Vice President for University Relations and Dean of College Enrollment	University of Chicago	mbehnke@uchicago.edu
Richard Bellows Executive Director Financial Aid	Butler University	bellows@butler.edu

James Belvin Director of Financial Aid	Duke University	jim.belvin@duke.edu
Julia Benz Director, Student Financial Services	Rice University	benz@rice.edu
Gail Berson Dean of Admission and Student Aid	Wheaton College	gberson@wheatoncollege.edu
Michael Beseda Vice Provost for Enrollment	Saint Mary's College of California	mbeseda@stmarys-ca.edu
Don Betterton Director of Financial Aid	Princeton University	dbett@princeton.edu
Deborah Bial President and Founder	The Posse Foundation	debbieb@possefoundation.org
Richard Bishop Director of Financial Aid and Admissions	Central Connecticut State University	bishopr@ccsu.edu
Patricia Bogart Senior Associate Director of Undergraduate Financial Aid	Duke University	pat.bogart@duke.edu
David Bousquet Vice President for Enrollment Management and Student Affairs	Northern Arizona University	david.bousquet@nau.edu
William Boyd Vice President for Enrollment Management and Student Affairs	San Diego State University	boyd12@mail.sdsu.edu
John Brady Vice President for Enrollment Management and Student Affairs	The College Board	jbrady@collegeboard.org
Sharon Brennan Director of Admissions and Enrollment Management	Southern Connecticut State University	brennan@southernct.edu
Steven Brooks Executive Director	North Carolina State Education Assistance Authority	sbrooks@ncseaa.edu
Charlene Brown Associate Director of Admissions	Albertson College of Idaho	cbrown@albertson.edu
Jane Brown Vice President for Enrollment and College Relations	Mount Holyoke College	jbbrown@mtholyoke.edu

Charles Bruce Senior Director, Office of Scholarships and Financial Aid	Oklahoma State University	charles.bruce@okstate.edu
Timothy Brunold Director and Associate Dean, Undergraduate Admission	University of Southern California	admdir@usc.edu
Kristine Butz Associate Director of Financial Aid	Butler University	kbutz@butler.edu
Larry Calderon President	Broward Community College	lcaldero@broward.edu
Paul Calme Director of Financial Aid	Xavier University	calme@xavier.edu
Wayne Camara Vice President, Research and Analysis	The College Board	wcamara@collegeboard.org
Marc Camille Dean of Admission	Xavier University	camille@xavier.edu
Gaston Caperton President	The College Board	gcaperton@collegeboard.org
Raul Cardenas Executive Director	Arizona State University	raul.cardenas@asu.edu
Robin Casanova Program Associate, CUES	The College Board	rcasanova@collegeboard.org
Joe Paul Case Dean and Director of Financial Aid	Amherst College	jpcase@amherst.edu
Arlene Cash Vice President for Enrollment Management	Spelman College	acash@spelman.edu
Jean Castruita Regional AVID Coordinator	AVID San Diego County Office of Education	2jcastru@sdcoe.net
David Charlow Executive Director, Financial Aid/Senior Associate Dean, Student Affairs	Columbia University	kgm11@columbia.edu
Debra Chermonte Dean of Admissions and Financial Aid	Oberlin College	debra.chermonte@oberlin.edu

Douglas Christiansen Assistant Vice President for Enrollment Management and Dean of Admissions	Purdue University	dlchristiansen@purdue.edu
Roderick Chu Chancellor	Ohio Board of Regents	rchu@regents.state.oh.us
Robert Clagett Dean of Admissions	Middlebury College	rclagett@middlebury.edu
Mark Clevenger Director of College and University Relations	Menlo School	mclevenger@menloschool.org
Chiara Coletti Vice President, Communications and Public Affairs	The College Board	ccoletti@collegeboard.org
Mary Contreras AVID Coordinator	AVID San Diego County Office Of Education	mcontrer@sdcoe.net
Youlonda Copeland-Morgan Vice President and Dean of Admission and Financial Aid	Harvey Mudd College	youlonda_copeland-morgan@hmc.edu
Patricia Covarrubias Assistant Professor of Communications and Journalism	University of New Mexico	pocb@unm.edu
Brian Cox Senior Vice President, Market Development	TERI/First Marblehead	bcox@fmd.com
Anne Deahl Associate Provost for Enrollment Management	Marquette University	anne.deahl@marquette.edu
John DeCourcy Director of Financial Aid	Washington and Lee University	jdecourcy@wlu.edu
Randall Deike Assistant Vice President, Undergraduate Education Executive Director, Undergraduate Admissions	Penn State University	rcd7@psu.edu; caw1@psu.edu
Jennifer Desjarlais Dean of Admission	Wellesley College	jdesjarl@wellesley.edu
Georgette DeVeres Associate Vice President of Admission and Financial Aid	Claremont McKenna College	georgette_deveres@mckenna.edu
Fred Dietrich Senior Vice President	The College Board	fdietrich@collegeboard.org
Robert Donaghey Assistant Director of Financial Aid	Dartmouth College	robert.donaghey@dartmouth.edu

Sally Donahue Director of Financial Aid	Harvard College	sdonahue@fas.harvard.edu
Kim Downs Director of Student Financial Services	Middlebury College	kdowns@middlebury.edu
Arthur Doyle Vice President, New England Region	The College Board	adoyle@collegeboard.org
Margaret Drugovich Vice President of Admission and Financial Aid	Ohio Wesleyan University	mldrugov@owu.edu
Michael Drummy Assistant Vice President, Enrollment Services	Chapman University	mdrummy@chapman.edu
Jane Edwards Director, International Programs	Harvard University	jedwards@fas.harvard.edu
Dolan Evanovich Vice Provost, Enrollment Management	University of Connecticut	dolan.evanovich@uconn.edu
John Fallon Chief Marketing Officer	The College Board	jfallon@collegeboard.org
Stephen Farmer Assistant Provost and Director of Undergraduate Admissions	University of North Carolina at Chapel Hill	smfarmer@email.unc.edu
Jean Farnsworth Associate Director, Financial Aid	Emory University	jdobson@emory.edu
Matthew Fissinger Director of Admission	Loyola Marymount University	mfissing@lmu.edu
William Fitzsimmons Dean of Admissions and Financial Aid	Harvard University	wrf@fas.harvard.edu
Adriana Flores-Ragade Manager, New SAT Outreach	The College Board	aflores@collegeboard.org
Jennifer Fondiller Dean of Admissions	Barnard College	jfondill@barnard.edu
Karen Fooks Director of Student Financial Affairs	University of Florida	kfooks@ufl.edu
Pamela Fowler Director of Financial Aid	University of Michigan	pfowler@umich.edu

Mabel Freeman Assistant Vice President, Undergraduate Admissions and First-Year Experience	The Ohio State University	freeman.9@osu.edu
Clint Gasaway Director of Financial Aid	Wabash College	gasawayc@wabash.edu
Barbara Gill Director, Undergraduate Admissions	University of Maryland	bgill@umd.edu
Daniel Goyette Director of Office of Student Financial Aid	Marquette University	dan.goyette@marquette.edu
Steven Graff Director and Senior Consultant, Admission and Enrollment Services	The College Board	sgraff@collegeboard.org
Larry Griffith Assistant Vice President, Higher Education Services	The College Board	lgriffith@collegeboard.org
Christopher Gruber Vice President and Dean of Admission and Financial Aid	Davidson College	chgruber@davidson.edu
Cynthia Gutierrez AVID Coordinator	AVID San Diego County Office of Education	cgutierrez@ocde.us
Reis Hagerman Higher Education Solutions Manager	The College Board	rhagerman@collegeboard.org
Stephen Handel National Director, Community College Initiatives	The College Board	shandel@collegeboard.org
Seamus Harreys Dean of Student Financial Services	Northeastern University	s.harreys@neu.edu
L. Katharine Harrington Dean of Admission and Financial Aid	University of Southern California	afadean@usc.edu
Natala Hart Director of Financial Aid	The Ohio State University	hart.149@osu.edu
Peter Hart Chief Executive Officer	Peter D. Hart Research Associates	lm@leadingauthorities.com
Cynthia Hartley Director of Graduate Student Aid Programs	Stanford University	chartley@stanford.edu

William Hartog Dean of Admissions and Financial Aid	Washington and Lee University	bhartog@wlu.edu
Hal Higginbotham President, collegeboard.com	The College Board	hhigginbotham@ collegeboard.org
Noel Hogan Vice President for Enrollment and Planning	Siena College	hogan@siena.edu
Don Honeman Dean of Admissions	University of Vermont	donald.honeman@uvm. edu
Pamela Horne Assistant to Provost for Enrollment Management and Director of Admissions	Michigan State University	pamhorne@msu.edu
Henry Ingle Vice Chancelor of Instructional Services, Planning, and Technology, and Online Education Programs	San Diego Community College System	hingle@sdccd.edu
Monica Inzer Dean of Admission and Financial Aid	Hamilton College	minzer@hamilton.edu
Janet Irons Associate Director of Financial Aid and Senior Admissions Officer	Harvard College	irons@fas.harvard.edu
Jennifer Jenkins Director of State Outreach	The College Board	jjenkins@collegeboard.org
Elizabeth Johnson Dean of Academic and Enrollment Services	University of San Francisco	johnson@usfca.edu
Ronald Johnson Director, Financial Aid	UCLA	rojohnso@saonet.ucla.edu
James Johnson Kenan Distinguished Professor	University of North Carolina Kenan-Flagler Business School	jim_johnson@unc.edu
David Jones Associate Dean for Admissions	University of Texas Medical School at San Antonio	jonesd@uthscsa.edu
Ned Jones Assistant Vice President for Enrollment Management	Siena College	jones@siena.edu
Michael Kabbaz Interim Chief Education Manager, Higher Education Services	The College Board	mkabbaz@collegeboard. org

Eva Kampits Director, Office of Executive Director	New England Association of Schools and Colleges, Inc. (NEASC)	kampits@neasc.org
Amelia Katanski Marlene Crandell Francis Assistant Professor of English	Kalamazoo College	amelia.katanski@kzoo.edu
Thomas Keane Director of Financial Aid for Scholarships and Policy Analysis	Cornell University	tck2@cornell.edu
Min Hee Kim Program Operations Coordinator	The College Board	mhkim@collegeboard.org
Steven Klein Dean of Admissions	Wabash College	kleins@wabash.edu
Saskia Knight Vice President and Dean of Enrollment Services	Chapman University	knight@chapman.edu
Jack Kopnsiky Chief Executive Officer and President	First Marblehead Corporation	jkopnisky@firstmarblehead.com
Sade Kosoko-Lasaki Associate Vice President, Health Science-Multicultural and Communication Affairs	Creighton University	skosoko@creighton.edu
Lori Kretten Associate Director of College Guidance	Cincinnati Hills Christian Academy	lori.kretten@chca-oh.org
Jenny Krugman Executive Director, College Board Partnerships	The College Board	jkrugman@collegeboard.org
Ann Larson Interim Director of Admission	Miami University	larsonal@muohio.edu
Mary Lou Lawyer Assistant Vice President for Financial Aid	Siena College	mlawyer@siena.edu
Robert Lay Dean for Enrollment Management	Boston College	lay@bc.edu
Joanne Letendre Director of College Counseling	Baylor School	joanne_letendre@baylorschool.org
Mark Lindenmeyer Director of Financial Aid	Loyola College in Maryland	lindenmeyer@loyola.edu

Kathleen Little Senior Executive Director, Financial Aid Programs and Services	The College Board	klittle@collegeboard.org
Judith Lewis Logue Director of Financial Aid Services	University of San Diego	jllogue@sandiego.edu
Jerome Lucido Vice Provost for Enrollment Policy and Management	University of North Carolina at Chapel Hill	jlucido@email.unc.edu
Deborah Luekens Senior Associate Director of Student Financial Services	Smith College	dluekens@smith.edu
Paula Luff Director of Financial Aid	DePaul University	pluff@depaul.edu
Matt Malatesta Director of Financial Aid	Hamilton College	mmalates@hamilton.edu
Hector Martinez Director of College Guidance	The Webb Schools	hmartinez@webb.org
Barry McCarty Dean of Enrollment Management	Lafayette College	mccartyb@lafayette.edu
James McCoy Associate Vice President for Enrollment Management	Xavier University	mccoy@xavier.edu
Heather McDonnell Director of Financial Aid	Sarah Lawrence College	hmdconn@sarahlawrence.edu
Christine McGuire Director, Office of Financial Aid	Boston University	chmcguir@bu.edu
Tom McKeon President and Chief Executive Officer	Tulsa Community College	tmckeon@tulsacc.edu
Sam McNair Executive Director of Admission and Enrollment Services	The College Board	smcnair@collegeboard.org
Thomas McWhertor Vice President for Enrollment and External Relations	Calvin College	mcwhto@calvin.edu
Nancy Meislahn Dean of Admission and Financial Aid	Wesleyan University	nmeislahn@wesleyan.edu

Lee Melvin Director of Undergraduate Admissions	University of Connecticut	lee.melvin@uconn.edu
Michael Mills Associate Provost, University Enrollment	Northwestern University	michael-mills@ northwestern.edu
Ron Moffat Director, International Student Center	San Diego State University	rmoffatt@mail.sdsu.edu
David Mohning Director of Student Financial Aid and Assistant Professor	Vanderbilt University	d.mohning@vanderbilt.edu
James Montoya Vice President of Higher Education, Assessments, Services, and Regions	The College Board	jmontoya@collegeboard. org
Warren Muller Dean of Admissions	Albertson College of Idaho	wmuller@albertson.edu
Susan Murphy Associate Dean, Academic and Enrollment Services	University of San Francisco	murphy@usfca.edu
Lynn Nichelson Director of Financial Aid	Illinois Wesleyan University	lnichels@titan.iwu.edu
Stefanie Niles Dean of Admission	DePauw University	sniles@depauw.edu
Erica O'Neal Assistant Vice President for Student Affairs	California Institute of Technology	eoneal@caltech.edu
Mary Nucciarone Assistant Director, Student Financial Services	University of Notre Dame	mnucciar@nd.edu
Stuart Oremus Director, College Counseling	The Wellington School	oremus@wellington.org
Gary Orfield Professor of Education and Social Policy	Harvard Graduate School of Education	orfielga@gse.harvard.edu
Shirley Ort Associate Provost and Director of Scholarships and Student Aid	University of North Carolina at Chapel Hill	sao@unc.edu
Peter Osgood Director of Admission	Harvey Mudd College	peter.osgood@hmc.edu

Rodney Oto Associate Dean of Admissions and Director of Student Financial Services	Carleton College	roto@acs.carleton.edu
Tony Pace Senior Educational Manager, Higher Education Services	The College Board	tpace@collegeboard.org
Julia Padgett University Director of Financial Aid	Emory University	jperrea@emory.edu
Thomas Parker Dean of Admission and Financial Aid	Amherst College	thparker@amherst.edu
Linda Peckham Director, Communication and Training	The College Board	lpeckham@collegeboard.org
Bernard Pekala Director of Financial Strategies	Boston College	pekala@bc.edu
Bruce Poch Vice President and Dean of Admissions	Pomona College	bruce.poch@pomona.edu
Barbara Porter Assistant Dean for Student Affairs	May Medical School	porter.barbara@mayo.edu
Stephen Pultz Director of Admission and Enrollment Management	University of San Diego	spultz@sandiego.edu
Bradley Quin Executive Director, CUES Operations and Support Services	The College Board	bquin@collegeboard.org
Janet Rapelye Dean of Admission	Princeton University	jrapelye@princeton.edu
Heather Renault Director of Admissions	Siena College	hrenault@siena.edu
Alicia Reyes Director of College Aid	University of Chicago	a-reyes@uchicago.edu
Molly Roebker Director of College Guidance	Cincinnati Hills Christian Academy	molly.roebker@chca-oh.org
Gerard Rooney Vice President, Enrollment Management and External Relations	St. John Fisher College	grooney@sjfc.edu

Mary Ann Rowan Vice President of Enrollment Management	Illinois Institute of Technology	rowan@iit.edu
Joseph Russo Director, Student Financial Strategies	University of Notre Dame	russo.4@nd.edu
Mary San Agustin Director of Financial Aid and Scholarships	Palomar College	msanagustin@palomar. edu
Daniel Saracino Assistant Provost for Enrollment	University of Notre Dame	saracino.3@nd.edu
William Schilling Director, Student Financial Aid	University of Pennsylvania	schilling@sfs.upenn.edu
Deb Schmidt Consultant	DTS Associates	dtsco@msn.com
Mary Carroll Scott Vice President, Membership	The College Board	mcscott@collegeboard.org
Alison Segal College Counselor	Highland Park High School	asegal@dist113.org
Dorothy Sexton Vice President and Secretary	The College Board	dsexton@collegeboard.org
Richard Shaw Dean, Undergraduate Admission and Financial Aid	Stanford University	lorettad@stanford.edu
Anne Shea Vice President for Enrollment and Student Affairs	Boston University	ashea@bu.edu
Joellen Silberman Dean of Enrollment	Kalamazoo College	silbermn@kzoo.edu
James Slattery Chief Educational Manager, Higher Education Services	The College Board	jslattery@collegeboard. org
Audrey Smith Dean of Enrollment	Smith College	aysmith@smith.edu
Brian Smith Senior Associate Director of College Counseling	Baylor School	brian_k_smith@ baylorschool.org

Lawrence Smith Vice President, Information Services and Enrollment Management	Mount St. Mary's College	lsmith@msmc.la.edu
Myra Smith Executive Director, Financial Aid Services	The College Board	msmith@collegeboard.org
Brian Spittle Assistant Vice President, Enrollment Management	DePaul University	bspittle@depaul.edu
Elizabeth Stanley Chief Educational Manager, Higher Education Services	The College Board	estanley@collegeboard.org
Lee Stetson Dean of Admission	University of Pennsylvania	angelas@admissions.upenn.edu
Caesar Storlazzi University Director of Financial Aid	Yale University	caesar.storlazzi@yale.edu
Forrest Stuart Director of Financial Aid	Rhodes College	stuart@rhodes.edu
Anne Sturtevant Director, Financial Aid Solutions	The College Board	asturtevant@collegeboard.org
Laura Talbot Director of Financial Aid	Swarthmore College	ltalbot1@swarthmore.edu
Catherine Thomas Associate Dean and Director Enrollment Services and Financial Aid	University of Southern California	ccthomas@usc.edu
Ronne Turner Dean of Admissions	Northeastern University	r.clement@neu.edu
John Volpini Senior Vice President of Business Development	First Marblehead Corporation	jvolpini@firstmarblehead.com
Richard Vos Vice President, Dean of Admission and Financial Aid	Claremont McKenna College	rvos@claremontmckenna.edu
Kelly Walter Executive Director of Admissions	Boston University	kwalter@bu.edu
Christopher Watson Director of Admission	Princeton University	cwatson@princeton.edu

William Wells Director of Financial Aid	Wake Forest University	wellswt@wfu.edu
Patricia White College Counselor	Summit Country Day	white_p@summitcds.org
Lucia Whittelsey Director of Financial Aid	Colby College	lwwhitte@colby.edu
Ken Woods Chief Education Manager, Higher Education Services	The College Board	kwoods@collegeboard.org
Andrew Workman Associate Provost	Mills College	aworkman@mills.edu
Ann Wright Vice President, Southwestern Region	The College Board	awright@rice.edu
Kris Zavoli Director, Regional Initiatives	The College Board	kzavoli@collegeboard.org